MINEHEAD (Route 8)

Preface

My wife and I have spent many happy days exploring Exmoor and the Quantocks. When we had our young family with us we found that Lynton provided a very pleasant base, particularly for Exmoor, and had several holidays there, even being recruited on one holiday to judge the fancy dress competition. As I write this, my children are scattered around the world and it has brought back many happy memories. There are particularly fond memories of the cream teas at Lee Bay provided by the Abbey's tea rooms, and at the National Trust tea rooms at Watersmeet. I hope that the book introduces many families to the pleasures that we experienced in the area.

HEDDONS MOUTH

About the author

John Caswell is a civil engineer. He was born and has lived most of his life in the Midlands but now lives in Somerset surrounded by the wonderful walking country of the south west of England. He has spent many weekends or longer holidays walking by himself or with family or friends in many parts of Great Britain; sometimes scrambling up the mountains of Wales or the Lake District or ski-ing in Scotland. His greatest pleasures are walking and music and he makes a valiant attempt to extract music from both the piano and the flute.

FAMILY WALKS

on

EXMOOR

and the

QUANTOCKS

John Caswell

Scarthin Books, Cromford, Derbyshire 1991.

FAMILY WALKS
ON EXMOOR AND THE QUANTOCKS

Family Walks Series
General Editor: Norman Taylor

———————

THE COUNTRY CODE
Enjoy the countryside and respect its life and work
Guard against all risk of fire
Fasten all gates
Keep your dogs under close control
Keep to public paths across farmland
Use gates and stiles to cross fences, hedges and walls
Leave livestock, crops and machinery alone
Take your litter home
Help to keep all water clean
Protect wildlife, plants and trees
Take special care on country roads
Make no unnecessary noise

———————

Published 1991

Phototypesetting, printing by Higham Press Ltd., Shirland, Derbyshire

ISBN 0 907758 46 0

CONTENTS

MAP OF THE AREA

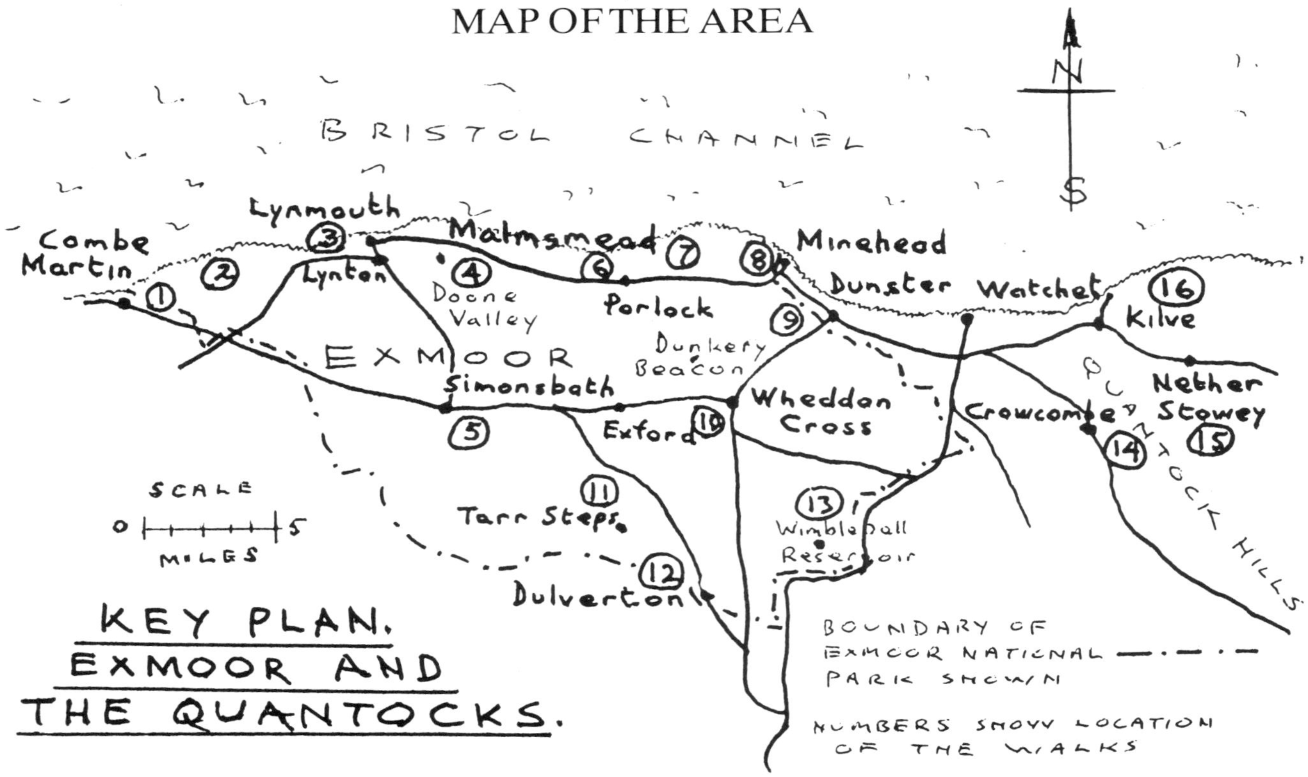
N
S
BRISTOL CHANNEL
Combe Martin
Lynmouth
Lynton
Malmsmead
Doone Valley
EXMOOR
Porlock
Minehead
Dunster
Watchet
Kilve
Nether Stowey
Crowcombe
QUANTOCK HILLS
Dunkery Beacon
Simonsbath
Exford
Wheddon Cross
Tarr Steps
Dulverton
Wimbleball Reservoir
1
2
3
4
5
6
7
8
9
10
11
12
13
14
15
16
SCALE
0
5
MILES
BOUNDARY OF EXMOOR NATIONAL PARK SHOWN
NUMBERS SHOW LOCATION OF THE WALKS
KEY PLAN.
EXMOOR AND
THE QUANTOCKS.

Introduction

The walks described in this book are set in a land of glorious contrasts straddling the Devon - Somerset border embracing Exmoor, the Quantocks and their coastal fringe.

The Quantocks, with their flanks covered in wooded combes, sweep up from the coast to 1260 feet at Will's Neck. Their tops, covered in bracken and heather are less dramatic than Exmoor, and more friendly. Along the top is a prehistoric ridgeway, at one point lined on both sides with beeches. The foot of the Quantocks is sprinkled with delightful villages. Coleridge lived at Nether Stowey with its main street bordered by a stream dotted with little bridges and Wordsworth enthused about the area. Picturesque East Quantoxhead, with its thatched cottages, duck pond, church and Jacobean Court House, is only yards from a fascinating coast studded with ammonites and where the underlying shales gave rise to a very early oil exploration industry, the only remains of which is the retort house preserved at Kilve.

The walks explore the back alleyways and the interesting quarters of the towns often missed by the casual tourist. Minehead is a town of contrasts with its quaint harbour and Church Town set alongside the modern holiday resort, which is now the terminus of the West Somerset Railway. Dunster has its "secret" garden and towering castle, while nowhere is more picturesque than Selworthy Green; nearby Porlock is a focal point of coast and country where the combes run down to the sea. Lynton and Lynmouth, linked by a charming cliff railway are flanked by dramatic coast and backed by wooded valleys and barren heights. Here the scale and nature of Exmoor is stunningly encapsulated in the pictures and other exhibits at Lynmouth showing the damage in August 1952 when torrential rain on Exmoor caused devastation alongside the rivers, and cost many lives.

The story of Lorna Doone is set in this area and centres on Badgworthy Water; various sites in the area are reputed to be the home of the Doones or elsewhere their graves, and many places are woven into Blackmore's text.

Exmoor National Park has a dramatic coastline with superb views across the Bristol Channel to the Welsh Coast and mountains. In many places the cliffs are unstable, as Exmoor lies on the Devonian beds of shale, slate and sandstone, though it has no large expanse of blanket bog. The wild, high moorland rises to 1703 feet at Dunkery Beacon, cloaked in heather and sculpted by fast flowing streams and rivers. The lower valleys are wooded, the high moor bare but not barren; inspiring, exhilarating, eerie in mist.

Maps designate the area "Exmoor Forest" which can be misleading; "Forest" meant land used for hunting, not in agricultural use, and subject to forest law. Due to cultivation the natural moor is now limited to the highest land.

The area covered by the book is sprinkled with prehistoric barrows and cairns, stone circles, iron age forts and Roman fortlets.

This is the territory of the red deer and Exmoor Pony; move quietly, keep a sharp look out, and you can be rewarded with sights of these and of many other birds and animals. Buzzards circle gracefully overhead with their distinctive "pee-oo" call, skylarks serenade the sky, meadow pipits flit from their nests in the grass and heather to scurry around you. Nearer the sea you may hear the "honk" of the raven or see them in a display of upside-down flying. Along the rivers you may glimpse the flash of blue of the kingfisher as it zips along, or watch the dance of the dippers while the salmon thread the waters.

The walks

All walks have been chosen to suit the needs of a family although all are equally enjoyable by walkers of any age or disposition, in groups or alone. There is much to absorb the lone walker and plenty to occupy the family en-route, rivers, streams, woods, picnic spots, old forts and stone circles; sometimes, rocks and beaches. All are in beautiful surroundings and you will discover a wealth of flora and fauna.

The scale of the landscape to some extent dictates the length of the walks, although many have shorter variations, and where small children or less experienced walkers are involved, it may be best to sample these shorter options first.

Pace and timing

A group of fast walkers rarely average more than 2½ miles in an hour allowing for gates, stiles, and pauses to appreciate the scenery. Young children may manage much less, and hill climbing will add further time. With small children one must always be prepared to turn back to avoid spoiling everyone's fun.

Clothing

It is difficult to give specific advice on the best type of clothing for these walks as they range from a seaside stroll to the heights of Exmoor, and though most will be done in Summer, I am sure some will sample the delights of walking in Winter and Spring when the area is just as attractive, and so much quieter.

Comfortable footwear is essential. It must be waterproof for walking in the moors, although no doubt, many will find stout trainers adequate for the lower walks nearer the coast. Thin soles offer less protection against rough surfaces although the soles of some walking boots may be too rigid; try several before buying, preferably wearing two pairs of socks, one thick and one thin.

Waterproofs range from the cheap non-breathing materials to those claimed to be fully permeable to water vapour and impermeable to rain, thus avoiding problems of sweat condensing inside. Opinions vary widely on the efficiency of these fabrics. The most ardent supporter I have met of the breathable type concedes that in long periods of heavy rain he does experience condensation on the inside. The non-breathable are in general cheaper, and lighter.

Warmth is essential especially on the more exposed walks on cliff tops or open moorland. This can best be achieved with several thin layers topped with a windproof layer. Most heat is lost through the head and a woolly hat is a great asset.

All spare clothing can be wrapped in a plastic bag (to keep dry) and carried in a rucksack.

Literature

People from all over the world come to Exmoor to see the places mentioned in the book by Richard Blackmore "Lorna Doone". Many people believe that the book is not a novel but based on the exploits of a band of robbers who terrorised the Exmoor area in the 17th century. Reading the book can be an interesting prelude to your holiday.

Henry Williamson's book "Tarka the Otter" relates the life of an otter in the country of the two rivers (slightly to the West of the area covered by this book). The Tarka Project is the theme for a number of initiatives, one of which is a footpath linking Lynton to Bideford. Another is "The Tarka Line" the British Rail route linking Barnstaple to Exeter which could provide an interesting day out when weather drives you from the walks.

Public Transport

The nearest British Rail stations are Bridgwater, Taunton and Barnstaple. The private West Somerset Railway runs along the foot of the Quantocks between Minehead and Bishops Lydeard with a bus connection between Bishops Lydeard and Taunton. There are stations at

Crowcombe, Williton, Watchet, Dunster and Minehead with some smaller intermediate stops.

Buses link the following:-

Bridgwater-Nether Stowey

Taunton-Crowcombe-Watchet-Dunster-Minehead

Dunster-Minehead-Porlock-Porlock Weir

Lynton-Barnstaple

Under current legislation buses are either provided as a normal commercial operation where an operator thinks it to be profitable or provided as a subsidised service by the County Council and operated by the person putting in the lowest (generally) tender. Services are in a state of flux and only the County Council can provide current details of the many operators in the area.

There are services in addition to those listed above but they are generally seasonal, very infrequent, often running only one day per week and generally of little use to the walker.

Enquiries should be directed to:-

Devon County Council or Somerset County Council

Exeter   Taunton

Bus Timetables can often be obtained from the Tourist Information Offices.

Fyne Court — Quantock Hills Information

Fyne Court is property owned by the National Trust and managed by the Somerset Trust for Nature Conservation who have provided nature trails and longer walks in the locality. There is an information centre and it is the base for the Quantock Hills Warden Service (Tel. Kingston St. Mary 526).

It is situated at the East end of the Quantocks at Broomfield near Bridgwater (G.R.222321).

Exmoor National Park Information

The following office is open all year round:-

Exmoor House,

Dulverton,

Somerset. Tel. 0398 23841.

Other offices are open during the tourist season at Dunster, County Gate, Lynmouth and Combe Martin.

There are tourist offices in towns operating independent from the Exmoor National Park.

8

Symbols used on the route maps

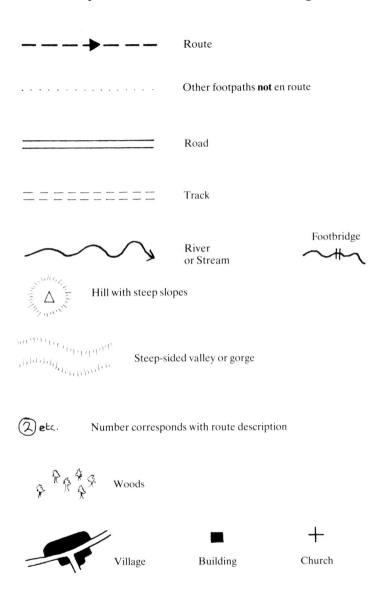

— — — ➤ — — —   Route

. . . .   Other footpaths **not** en route

══════════   Road

═ ═ ═ ═ ═ ═ ═ ═ ═ ═   Track

River
or Stream

Footbridge

Hill with steep slopes

Steep-sided valley or gorge

② etc.   Number corresponds with route description

Woods

Village   Building   Church

9

A SECRET GARDEN (Route 9)

Combe Martin and Great Hangman

Outline   Combe Martin sea front car park ~ Clorridge Hill ~ Parish Church ~ Holland Park ~ Great Hangman ~ Coast Path ~ Little Hangman ~ Combe Martin.

Summary   A walk combining town, seaside and country; the first part is more sheltered yet giving a panoramic view over Combe Martin and exploring the quieter corners of the town including the gardens set beside the stream; the second part reaches the high cliffs above the town before descending along the coast path.

Attractions   Around Combe Martin one can still see evidence of the strip field system and ruins of the silver and tin mines. "The hunting of the Earl of Rone" was a ceremony that became so riotous that it was banned in 1837; it has now been resurrected and takes place on Spring Bank Holiday.

After parking, you may have difficulty dragging some of the family away from the beach and the stream which runs down the combe on to the beach. Other members of the family may be diverted by the Motor Cycle Museum which lies just to the left of the exit from the car park.

Soon, the walk drops into a sheltered combe filled with a variety of wild plants including the pungent wild garlic before leaving the stream and climbing to a vantage point on Cloridge Hill. To the left lies Combe Martin Bay, below is the town straggling along two miles in the bottom of the combe. In the distance is Little Hangman on the left and Great Hangman on the right. Nearer than Hangman is Knap Down, with the mine chimney clearly visible still. Below the church the streamside gardens are an ideal picnic spot.

On reaching the main road (Point 3) a few yards to the left is The Pack of Cards public house, built by a man who won a lot at cards. It looks like a house of cards, and had 52 windows.

Beyond the main road, Holland Park is a grand play area. Rising up to Great Hangman the views improve with every step. The National Trust own both Great and Little Hangman and this is a fine adventure area with magnificent views and plenty of picnic space. A grand place for kites.

The descent to Combe Martin presents different views at each turn and passes a tea shop set only yards from the cliff edge.

Refreshments   Combe Martin offers a wide choice of refreshment stops.

Route 1

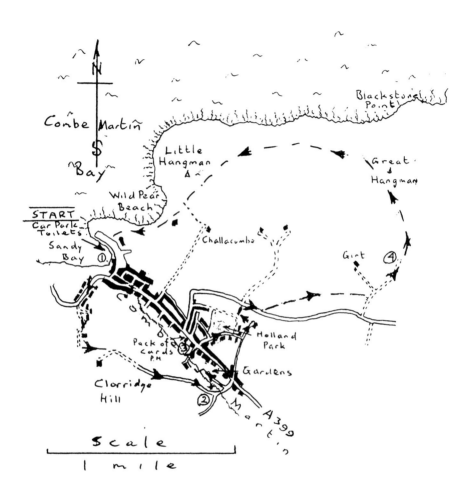

Route 1

Combe Martin and Great Hangman

6½ miles

(Shorter variation 3 miles)

START *At the sea front car park/toilets at Combe Martin (G.R.577475).*

ROUTE

1. *From the car park walk to the main road and turn right along the main road to follow it as it rises up from the sea, bends to the left and then straightens out. At the end of the straight length, turn left down to the stream. Follow the stream, then the valley, along the winding drive. Climb a stile at the end and turn left in the field.*
   Climb up the field keeping the hedge on your left and maintain this same direction as you enter the next field and reach a track. Follow the track downhill to the church.

2. *Walk beside the boundary wall of the church then follow the stream through the car park and into the public gardens (keeping to the right through the car park). Bear left in the gardens to cross the footbridge and, with the stream on your right, continue to the cottages on the left hand edge of the path. At the end of which, turn right along the drive to meet the main road.*

3. *Cross the main road, bearing slightly to the right to climb up from the main road with the post office on the left and the chapel on the right into Chapel Lane. Follow Chapel Lane uphill (passing Holland Park on your left) and continue to follow it as it bears right. The lane finishes at a 'T' junction with a lane to the right and a footpath to the left. Turn left up the footpath, then left at the next 'T' junction to follow a path in a deep cleft, which swings right and uphill. Turn right on to the tarmac road and, after 50 yards, fork left along a path signposted "Knap Down Lane and Great Hangman". At the end of the path bear left on to the lane and follow it for ¼ mile to the gate at the end.*

4. *Keep the hedge on the right, maintain this direction until you meet the Coast Path passing the National Trust boundary sign "Great Hangman". Bear left on to the Coast Path and follow it down to the sea front at Combe Martin.*

SHORTER VARIATION

At point 3 follow the main road down to the sea front.

PETER'S CLIFF

14

Hunter's Inn, Heddon's Mouth Cleave

Outline   Hunter's Inn ~ Heddon's Mouth Cleave ~ Peter's Cliff ~ Trentishoe ~ Mill Farm ~ Hunter's Inn.

Summary   The walk explores the beautiful valley of the River Heddon below Parracombe and includes an exhilarating cliff walk.

Attractions   Hunter's Inn has a beautiful setting in the midst of sessile oak woods which rise up to cliff tops covered in colourful ling, heather and gorse. In the woods are wood warblers and redstarts while on the cliffs you can see razorbills and guillemots. The whole area is protected by the National Trust and is quite idyllic.

The riverside path through the woods is a delight for all ages and most families will be unable to resist an excursion to the beach after crossing the footbridge. It is a delightful beach, with plenty of flat stones to skim across the water; at one corner is an old lime kiln where lime from across the channel in South Wales was burnt to provide quicklime for the surrounding area.

At Trentishoe you can make the trip up the hill to the church which still has the musician's gallery at the rear of the church with a display of the instruments which they played before the use of the organ. In 1867 they had their first organ installed but the parishoners were not asked to subscribe as they would have expected to join in the singing. Blackmore (the author of Lorna Doone) used the village as the setting for his novel Clara Vaughan.

The walk around Peter's Cliff is very exciting for older children but **families with younger children may wish to avoid this section.**

If you venture to the station tea garden (see below) you must look inside Saint Petrock's church next door. It is not used and the interior is just as it was 200 years ago.

Refreshments   A variety of refreshments can be purchased at the shop next to the car park at Hunter's Inn and from the Inn itself.

Up the valley at Parracombe the Station Tea Garden and railway walk provides teas etc. on the site of the Lynton and Barnstaple Railway. There is also an inn at Parracombe. (G.R.675450 and 668448 respectively).

Route 2

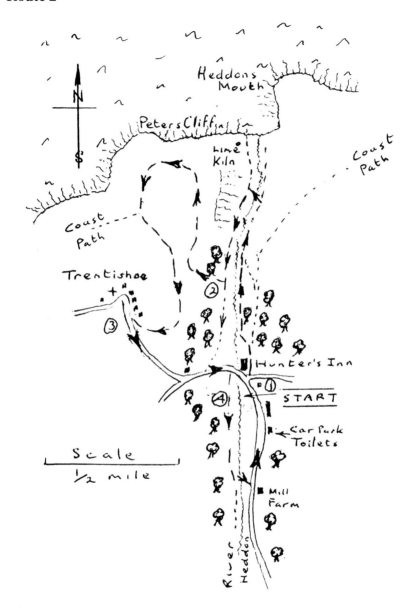

Route 2

Hunter's Inn, Heddon's Mouth Cleave   **4 miles**

(Shorter variation 2 miles)

START   *From the car park/toilets at Hunter's Inn (G.R.655480). Hunter's Inn is signposted off the A39 at Parracombe and off the A399 at Combe Martin.*

ROUTE

1. *Walk past the inn, keeping the inn on your left. Fork left and fork left again to follow the river on your left. Turn left over the footbridge and follow the path from the bridge to meet the main path after a few yards, then turn left to walk back up the valley. Enter the woodland, pass through a gate.*

2. *Turn sharp right off the broad path to climb steeply up through the woods then beyond the woods up the open hillside. Turn right to follow the path as it levels out half way up the hill and walk towards the sea. Follow the path as it bends to the left along the face of Peter's Cliff above the sea and then turn left away from the sea, to rise up to a fence. Do not follow the Coast Path to the right here but turn left to walk inland, keeping the fence on your right. Soon the River Heddon comes into view again, but now down below on your left as you approach Trentishoe. Continue to a tarmac lane.*

3. *Turn left down the tarmac lane (unless you wish to visit the church) and walk downhill. Bear left at the road junction to return towards Hunter's Inn.*

4. *Just before the Inn, turn right and follow the path, keeping the river on the left. After ½ mile cross the river, bear right across the field to leave through a gate, and turn left along the lane to return to the Inn.*

SHORTER VARIATIONS

At point 2, do not turn uphill, but continue along the level, broad path to meet the road then turn left towards the Inn.

NOTE

(a) *Those who wish to avoid the cliff path should not take the right hand path above point 2 but carry on up to the fence at the top of the hill above point 2 and turn left to Trentishoe.*

(b) *From Point 2 to just beyond Peter's Cliff, the route follows what is now the coast path along National Trust Property, although older maps will show the Coast Path as running from Trentishoe towards Peter's Cliff.*

LYNMOUTH AND THE CLIFF RAILWAY

Route 3   3¾ miles

Lynton, Valley of the Rocks, Lee Bay

Outline   Lynton ~ Hollerday Hill ~ Cricket Ground ~ Valley of the Rocks ~ Lee Bay ~ Cliff Path ~ Lynton.

Summary   A picturesque walk affording panoramic views over the sea, Lynmouth Bay and this part of the North Devon coast. The route follows paths except for a short stretch of toll road belonging to Lee Abbey. The initial ascent is gradual and the highest point can be by-passed if so desired.

Attractions   Lynmouth lies at the junction of the East and West Lyn rivers and it is connected to its higher twin town of Lynton by the cliff railway. This was built in 1890 and the walk starts from the top station.

The Valley of the Rocks Hotel reaches out across the main street seemingly to try and touch the buildings opposite; steps lined with shops lead down to Queen Street and the Lyn and Exmoor Museum. The attractive Town Hall houses the Tourist Office and over the road you can try and toss a coin into the basket for the local cottage hospital.

Above the Town Hall, where there is a fine view over Lynmouth Bay towards Countisbury, the cars negotiating the 1 in 4 hill appear like Dinky toys against the magnificent backdrop of Exmoor which terminates with the lighthouse on Foreland Point. Those who reach the highest point (and don't take the short cut on the lower route) will be rewarded with a 360° panorama from the top of Hollerday Hill encompassing the Welsh coast to the North across the Bristol Channel, the nearby coastal fringe of Exmoor and to the South views over Lynton towards Exmoor.

The descent down the West side of the hill offers a magnificent view of the amphitheatre which is the Valley of the Rocks. Grotesque rock formations soar up from the valley floor. To the right stands Castle Rock, Rugged Jack and Chimney Rock, to the left the Devil's Cheesewring towers above Mother Meldrum's Cave.

The valley features in the famous novel Lorna Doone. Mother Meldrum, the seer, sheltered within the Devil's Cheesewring and here John Ridd, the hero of the tale, watched the fight between a goat and the sheep; he also noticed the wonderful echoes. Now when the air is still you can stand on one side of the valley and hear your echo bounce from the opposite rocks. It is possible to climb Castle Rock with care though you

continued on page 22

19

Route 3

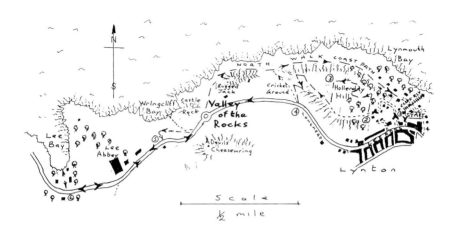

Scale
½ mile

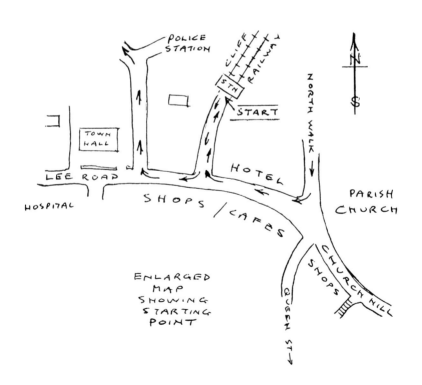

ENLARGED
MAP
SHOWING
STARTING
POINT

Route 3

Lynton, Valley of the Rocks, Lee Bay   3¾ miles
(Shorter variation 2½ miles)

START   *From Lynton Cliff Railway Station (G.R.719496) off Lea Road. Car park at Church Hill at the East end of Lee Road.*

ROUTE

1. *Leave the station, turn right into Lee Road and first right at the Town Hall. Take the left fork and follow the track as it bends to the left, then turn sharp left at the next junction.*

2. *After the track bends to the right, take the second turn on the right signed "To the Picnic Area" (just past a bungalow on the left). Ignore the next left forks and, at the far end of the picnic area/viewpoint, turn left up the steps with the handrail, then take the right hand fork (signed "Valley of the Rocks"). Follow this path as it bends right, then left, with the cliff edge wall now on the right and a gap in a wall ahead. Keep to the main path to pass through the gap in the wall ahead (not the gap towards the cliff edge) then through the next wall gap. (Hollerday Hill summit is up on your right).*

3. *At this gap, turn left on to the broad path downhill then sharp right (signed "Valley of the Rocks"). Turn left downhill before the cliff edge and follow the path as it zig zags down to the road.*

4. *Turn right on to the road, follow it to the roundabout and then for 100 yards beyond to turn right along the path (avoid the path on the right leading down to Wringcliff Bay). At the boundary of Lee Abbey Farm turn left up to the road.*

5. *Turn right on to the road and follow it down to Lee Bay.*

6. *Return along the road to point 5, then remain on the road if you wish to view "The White Lady". Continue to the roundabout and bear left to follow the Coast Path as far as the bridge over the cliff railway. From the railway follow the lane ahead, which then bends to the right and rises to Lee Road. Turn right to pass in front of the hotel and right again to the Cliff Railway Station.*

SHORTER VARIATION

At point 2, if you wish to avoid further climbing, do not turn right but continue straight ahead to rejoin the route below point 3.

     At point 4 turn sharp right along a path past a cricket ground to meet the Coast Path, then right again, along the Coast Path. Return to the Cliff Railway Station as in Stage 6.

may find yourself sharing your lofty perch with one of the goats which inhabit the valley. From a viewpoint on the road you can see the opening in Castle Rock which is the "White Lady".

Lee Bay has a charming tea shop, with a small customer's library; and a small natural history museum on the estate of the Lee Abbey, a Christian retreat centre.

The coast path has breath-taking views of the sea below where you may see the crab pot floats bobbing in the sea or even the occasional seal.

On a narrow bridge over the cliff railway one can stand and watch the Emmett-like carriage rise and fall along the 1 in 1¾ track between Lynton and Lynmouth. You can hear the bell signals as the carriages are ready to start and the rush of water as the top tank fills and the weight of the top carriage with its tank full of water starts to pull the lower one uphill. The passengers on the open end wave or click their cameras as they glide beneath your feet.

The railway, the hospital and the Town Hall were largely the result of the efforts of fund raising by Sir George Newnes, the publisher, whose house stood in the grounds of Hollerday Hill through which the walk passes.

Refreshments   There are several cafés in Lynton and Lynmouth as well as hotels and also cafés at Lee Bay and the Valley of the Rocks.

CLOUD FARM

22

Route 4

Malmsmead, Oare Church, Lorna Doone Valley

Outline   Malmsmead ~ Oare Church ~ South Common ~ Badgworthy Water ~ Lank Combe Waterslide ~ Cloud Farm ~ Malmsmead.

Summary   The walk explores the country which is central to the legend of the Doones. It rises from the valley of Oare Water to the high heather covered moor at 1334 feet before following Badgworthy Water down into the shelter of the Doone Valley.

Attractions   Before setting off it is fun to linger at Malmsmead and watch the cars and horses splash through the ford beside the lovely bridge. The high moorland can be quite an adventure and there are lots of waterside spots for a picnic, paddling, or games, and lovely woodland around Lank Combe for hide and seek.

   The walk can best be appreciated by those who have read the story of Lorna Doone. Lank Combe is the real Doone Valley where the family of robbers (the Doones) lived and held Lorna (who incidentally was not a Doone) as their hostage for many years until rescued by John Ridd. Here you will see the waterslide where John Ridd climbed up and met the beautiful Lorna.

   Hoccombe Combe contains the remains of houses which some authors say are those of the Doones but most evidence would preclude that as a possibility.

   After the daring rescue John Ridd married Lorna, but alas, after placing the ring on her finger, as John was about to kiss her, a shot rang out, and her eyes were full of death. You can see the scene of the crime in Oare Church, why not read the rest of the story?

Refreshments   Light refreshments are available at Malmsmead and at Cloud Farm.

NOTE

At peak periods the narrow lanes and parking spaces may be crowded; if you wish you may park at the information centre at County Gate on the main A39 road and walk down marked paths to Malmsmead or Oare to join the walk.

Route 4

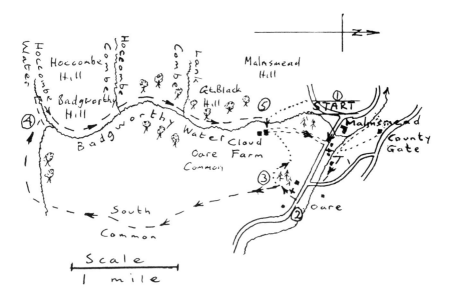

Hoccombe Water

Hoccombe Hill

Hoccombe Combe

Hoccombe Combe

Combe

Lank Combe

Gt. Black Hill

Malmsmead Hill

Badgworthy Hill

Badgworthy Water

START

Malmsmead

County Gate

④

Cloud Farm

Oare Common

⑤

Oare

①

③

②

South Common

Scale
1 mile

THE WATERSLIDE

24

Route 4

Malmsmead, Oare Church, Lorna Doone Valley   7 miles

(Shorter variation 3 miles)

START   *From the car park adjoining the river at Malmsmead (G.R.792477).*

ROUTE

1. *From the car park walk across the bridge and along the lane for 400 yards, then turn left down the drive to Lorna Doone and Parsonage Farm. Walk past the farmhouse and then down to the bridge. Cross the river and take the path on your right leading away from the river for 50 yards. Turn right to walk parallel with the river. Bear slightly left to stay outside the farm boundary fence. Where the path meets the road turn right to a 'T' junction. At the junction turn left and walk past the church.*

2. *Go through a gate on your right and walk through the field with the church on your right. Follow the hedge on your right through two fields to the third gate, where the hedge on the right is replaced with a fence, and ahead on the right is a small combe with a plantation of conifers.*

3. *At this gate, ignore the arrow and the path ahead (unless you are following the short variation). Follow the depression in the ground on the left and bear away from the main path at about 30° angle to follow the crest of the ridge rising up the field. Shortly, a wire fence comes into view on the left. Walk uphill and pass through a gate in the fence. Continue towards the top of the field, again passing through a gate in the fence. At the top of the field two hedges on earth banks meet at a right angle. Keep to the right of this hedge junction and walk ahead, keeping the hedge on your left. (Shortly after this point you will leave the grassland and then be walking on the heather covered moorland and, in many places, there is no clear path; a few minor deviations will be necessary to avoid muddy patches when crossing streams etc.) After about a mile, follow the hedge as its alignment turns 90° to the right at a small gate (don't pass through the gate but keep the hedge/bank on your left) and walk south for a further ¾ mile, to where the hedge terminates at the head of a combe. Here a stream rises and runs to the right. Cross the stream by the gate, turn right and follow the stream down to its confluence with the next river at Badgworthy Water and Hoccombe Water.*

4. *Cross Badgworthy Water and turn right to walk downstream (it may be necessary to first turn left to walk to the nearest footbridge 400 yards away). Follow the river downhill to Cloud Farm.*

25

5. *Cross the footbridge to the farm, turn left, and carry on downstream with the water now on your left until you meet the road at Malmsmead. Turn left to the bridge and the car park.*

SHORTER VARIATION

At point 3 follow the path ahead alongside the small combe with the conifers (on your right) and make a U-turn to the right at the head of the combe (Signed Doone Valley). Ascend to join another path, turn next left and continue ascending to a gate. Pass through the gate and follow the path as it swings to the left and drops to Cloud Farm (point 5). Turn right to follow the river.

SIMONSBATH

26

Simonsbath and Cow Castle

Outline   Simonsbath ~ Winstitchen ~ Picked Stones ~ Cow Castle ~ Wheal Eliza ~ Simonsbath.

Summary   A walk into the remote heart of Exmoor without a lot of climbing yet offering typical Exmoor landscape with a sheltered river valley for the return to Simonsbath.

Attractions   William I established Exmoor as a Royal Forest (Forest meant land protected as a hunting reserve and outside agricultural use, subject to forest law). In 1818 The Crown sold to John Knight, who with his son, established their farmstead of 15,500 acres here at Simonsbath. Attempts at mixed farming failed but Knight's son encouraged sheep farming and mined copper and iron. Typical Exmoor farmsteads are seen on this walk and the site of the disused Wheal Eliza Mine. Cow Castle is an iron age fort overlooking the River Barle and a great place for children to explore and use their imagination.

   The beech wood through which the walk passes at the start (Birchcleave Wood) was planted in 1840 and is believed to be the highest beech wood in England at 1100 ft. It makes a lovely adventure area for the children. Simonsbath House Hotel was originally the house of James Bovey who was the first commoner to obtain the freehold of the Exmoor Forest in 1652; the date 1652 is carved into one of its beams.

   The riverside provides a good choice of picnic and play areas and an opportunity to study the site of the old mine.

Refreshments   Simonsbath House Hotel provides the usual facilities including cream teas, similarly Exmoor House Hotel, both at Simonsbath.

Route 5

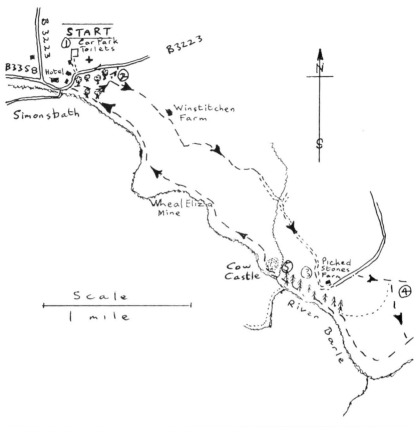

START ① Car Park Toilets
B3223
B3358
Hotel
②
Simonsbath
Winstitchen Farm
Wheal Elizia Mine
Cow Castle
③
Picked Stones Farm
④
River Barle

N
S

Scale
1 mile

Route 5

Simonsbath and Cow Castle

7 miles
(Shorter variation 1 mile)

START *From the car park/toilets off the B3223 below Simonsbath church (G.R.773393).*

ROUTE

1. *Walk back from the car park to the road, turn right, walk downhill past the hotel, cross the road and continue downhill for a few yards until you reach the bottom of the woodland. Enter the beech wood through the small gate and take the middle of the three paths to climb uphill and gradually bend to the left.*

2. *Where the path starts to descend, turn right through the gate to leave the wood and enter open fields with a hedge on your left, walking in a South East direction. At the next gate continue in the same direction, pass through it (ignore the gate on your right) and enter the next field with the hedge on your right. You meet a pair of gates in this hedgeline. Pass through the second, still maintaining the same direction (South East) but with the hedge on your left. At the next gate, where the ground starts to fall, study the route ahead, following the hedgeline as far as you can see. Follow that hedge with a short kink to the left at Winstitchen Farm. 400 yards beyond Winstitchen Farm, where the hedge bears to the right, turn left through the hedge, thus changing direction to walk East with a hedge on your left. After passing through a gap in an old hedge/bank bear left as the ground begins to fall (notice the path rising up the hillside beyond the valley) then turn right to follow the path alongside the gulley falling to the valley below. Cross the stream and turn right to follow the track up the hill to join and follow a hedge on your left.*

3. *At Picked Stones Farm turn left through the hedgeline (a conifer plantation is below you at this point) to enter the farmyard. Follow the lane leading uphill from the farm for 300 yards, and turn right through a gate. Follow the hedge on your right, passing straight ahead through a gate at the end of the field, to emerge on to the open moor.*

4. *Turn right to follow the open moor down to the river (Note; the public bridleway running through the enclosed farmland and down to the river is obstructed at this point so use the moorland route as directed). Turn right at the river to follow it towards Simonsbath, keeping the river on your left.*

29

5. *Emerging from the conifer wood, cross the small footbridge to approach the ancient earthwork which is Cow Castle. Beyond Cow Castle follow the river (keeping it on your left) to the mine site where the path turns right, leaving the river for a short distance. Follow the path along the river valley to the road at Simonsbath. Turn right on to the road to reach the car park.*

SHORTER VARIATION

At point 2, do not turn right but follow the path ahead through the wood to the road and turn left to return to the car park.

PORLOCK WEIR

Route 6

Porlock, Bossington, Porlock Weir

Outline   Porlock ~ Villes Lane ~ Bossington ~ Porlock Way ~ Porlock Weir ~ Porlock.

Summary   An ideal walk combining village, fields, woodland with a stroll along the shingle ridge adjoining Porlock Bay.

Attractions   Porlock is notorious for its 1 in 4 hill on the main A39 coast road with tortuous hairpin bends. For this reason heavy vehicles are banned. The main street with a pleasing mixture of houses, hotels, shops and cafes in a variety of styles is a pleasing prelude to the walk. The path to Bossington is lined with prolific blackberry bushes while Bossington offers a lovely selection of cafes.

The middle section traverses the long shingle ridge to Porlock Weir and offers great scope for children to let off steam; there is plenty of ammunition to throw at driftwood and plenty of waves and birds to watch.

From Porlock Weir an additional walk of 1½ miles along the coast path will take you to Culbone Church, the smallest church in England in regular use.

The return through the woods is a good spot for hide and seek or exploration. Although Bossington village lies slightly off the route it is worthwhile strolling down the village to look at the unusual style of houses and to study the tea shops.

Porlock church spire lost its top in a storm in the 17th century and is now a rather unusual shape. Nearby, the tourist information office is housed in a 15th century building which was probably a dowerhouse to Porlock Manor.

A row of 17th century cottages stand at Porlock Bay, built from rocks off the beach. Remains of a forest may be exposed at low tide.

Refreshments   A wide choice of refreshment is available at Porlock, Porlock Weir and Bossington.

Route 6

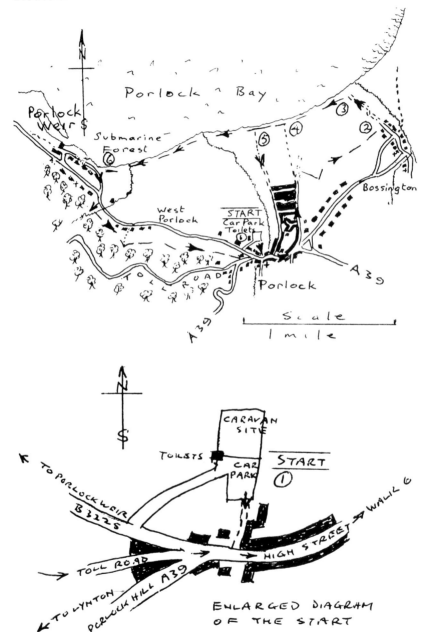

Route 6

Porlock, Bossington, Porlock Weir   **6 miles**

(Shorter variation 3 miles)

START   *At the car park/toilets at the West end of Porlock village (G.R.885489). The entrance to the car park is a few yards from the A39 road along the B3225 which leads to Porlock Weir.*

ROUTE

1. *Follow the footpath from the end of the car park which leads between the shops. Turn left to follow the main street for ¼ mile, then turn left into Villes Lane. Where this lane meets Bay Road take the right hand path, which leads to a stile. Do not cross this stile but follow the obvious path. On reaching another stile, cross it to enter the field with a hedge on your right, and cross a stile into the next field. Turn left to follow the hedge on your left and cross another stile, keeping the same hedge on your left. Pass through a gate in the hedge, maintaining the same direction but now with the hedge on your right and a second hedge on your left. As you reach the farm buildings, turn left and bend to the right to meet the tarmac lane.*

2. *Turn left into the lane and follow it as it turns right then left; then fork right to reach the beach.*

3. *Turn left to walk close to the hedge and parallel with the shore, until you reach a disused building at the start of the sea wall. Walk along the landward side of the sea wall (unless you choose to continue to walk along the beach).*

4. *Where the sea wall turns across your path, continue to the next stile (approximately 40 yards beyond the sea wall) and cross into the field. (Here a path leads off left back to Villes Lane). This location is marked on the beach with a large pointed stake. Continue walking through the field parallel with the beach.*

5. *At the second breakwater, (where a path leads left to the village), continue walking along the beach until you reach the sea wall at Porlock Weir.*

6. *Cross the sea wall and turn left along the road. After passing a lane on the right, and where the road bends to the left, leave the road and take the path ahead into the woods. Cross a narrow tarmac drive and continue into the woods with the stream on your left. Bear left alongside a large shed, take the left hand fork to the bridge, and cross the stream. Ascend the broad path (ignore the path which branches off to the right) and take the next left branch (Signed to Porlock). Follow this path,*

which runs along the lower edge of the woodland all the way to Porlock. However, after ¼ mile ignore a path which runs off down hill to West Porlock. When you emerge from the woods, turn left down the toll road and into the main village street to the entrance to the car park.

SHORTER VARIATION

At point 5, turn left to follow a path which leads into a lane and back to the main street, where you turn right to the car park. Do not walk in the narrow lane itself as, on the left hand side, a parallel higher path through the field gives a better view.

ALLERFORD

Bossington, Selworthy, Bossington Hill

Outline   Bossington ~ Allerford ~ Selworthy ~ Bossington Hill
Bossington.

Summary   A sheltered woodland walk calling on the delightful villages and then rising through beautiful woodland to the vantage point of Selworthy Beacon.

Attractions   No visit to Exmoor would be complete without a while in the villages of Bossington and Selworthy. Selworthy is a gem of whitewashed thatched cottages clustered around well maintained lawns and gardens and sheltering under the 15th century church, which is also quite beautiful inside. In the churchyard is a 14th century cross. The cottages were built in 1828 by the Acland family who also provided the scarlet coats for the pensioners who lived here. The Acklands lived at Exeter and acquired the Holnicote Estate by marriage in 1745 and used the area for hunting while staying at Holnicote House (on the A39 nearby).

Sir Richard Dyke Ackland gave the whole estate of 12400 acres to the National Trust including Dunkery Beacon the highest point of Exmoor. The hillside above Bossington has been planted at various times in the 19th century to commemorate births in the Ackland family. Many evergreen oaks were planted, these have leaves like holly but lighter in colour and are called "holm oaks"; holm is an old name for holly. Another unusual tree in this setting is cherry laurel.

In the woods are several reminders of the estate's earlier usage, memorial huts, crosses, Saint Agnes' Fountain, Catherine's Well, the iron age hill fort of Bury Castle and Selworthy Beacon which, at 1011 feet above the sea was used as a beacon to warn of the Spanish Armada; there are Bronze Age cairns and tumuli.

In Bossington most of the cottages are 17th century and have very large bases to the chimneys to contain the bread ovens. A mediaeval chapel stands next to the Farm Park and the Rural Life Museum is just down the road towards Allerford. Bossington car park has a picnic site bordering the River Aller and a toilet block.

The River Aller borders the walk at several points and offers a lovely diversion for children. The woods are a fine venue for 'hide and seek' and the heights of the Beacon are a grand place to play or just enjoy the view

continued on page 38

35

Route 7

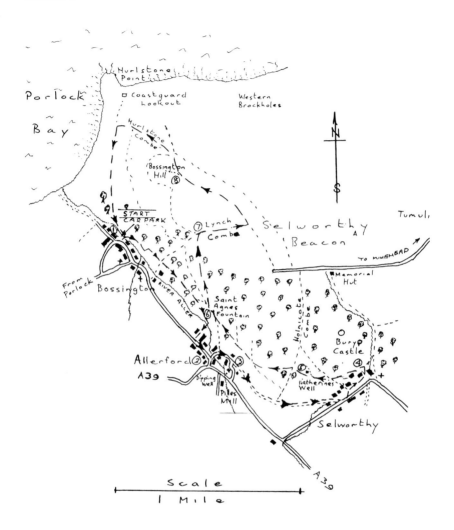

Route 7

Bossington, Selworthy, Bossington Hill.   6 miles

(Shorter variation 4 miles)

START   *At the car park/toilets/picnic site at the North West end of Bossington (G.R.898480).*

ROUTE

1. *From the car park, cross the footbridge over the river, fork right and fork right again to follow the river. Turn left into the field, then right after a few yards, to follow a hedge on your right, and enter the woods at the end of the field. Keep straight ahead at the crossing of the first path (where the path drops down to West Lynch and Horner). Fork right at the next junction downhill towards Allerford, then fork right and cross the stream and join a tarmac drive. Turn left on to the main village street and follow it to the pack horse bridge by the ford.*

2. *Turn left over the bridge, follow the road around to the right and then straight on for ¼ mile. Straight ahead is a stoney track and the road dropping down to the right to Piles Mill.*

3. *Take the track ahead to Selworthy, where it meets a tarmac road. Follow the road uphill and, immediately past the toilets (on the left), pass through a small gate on the left on to Selworthy Green and walk up the green passing the cafe and National Trust shop.*

4. *Leave the green going uphill, keeping the shop on your right. Cross the stream and turn left. After a few yards ignore the path which forks right and ignore the next left fork. Where the next path crosses take the path ahead to Allerford.*

5. *At Catherine's Well branch left to follow the edge of the wood to the crossing of the next path, keeping straight ahead towards Bossington (left leads down to Allerford, right leads up to North Hill). Keep straight on towards Bossington at the next crossing. At the next junction, where three paths fan out ahead, take the lower on the left towards Saint Agnes Fountain and Bossington.*

6. *At the fountain six paths meet. Take the right hand path (the high level path to Hurlestone Point), climbing and slowly curving to the right to pass through a small gate, where you join the path rising from the left up Lynch Combe. (Ignore the path on the left).*

7. *Follow the main path up the base of the combe, with the stream on your left, then on your right, until you emerge on the open hill top, where the narrow path from the combe meets a broad path running along the rim*

37

of the combe. Turn left towards the stone cairn which is visible ahead on Bossington Hill (Selworthy Beacon is on your right).

8. *About 100 yards before the cairn, ignore the left fork. Instead keep straight ahead to the head of the next combe (Hurlstone Combe), where six paths meet and a sign indicates a dangerous path ahead. Turn left to follow the Coast Path down the combe. At the end of the combe turn left at the fence and follow the path for ½ mile then bear right, over the river, to return to the car park.*

SHORTER VARIATION

At point 6 (Saint Agnes Fountain) take the lower path ahead to rejoin the outward route at the next junction and return to Bossington.

---

including Dunkery Beacon to the South, Foreland Point to the West, North to Wales (the distant lighthouse is Nash Point), East to Weston Super Mare and the Mendips. Bury Castle is another place for the imagination to play games; it comprises a 200 ft. diameter wall made of stone and earth, 10 ft. high, surrounded by a fosse on North and West sides, the ramparts having originally been topped with a wooden barrier.

At Allerford, beside the ford which crosses the River Aller, is a 15th century pack horse bridge. Piles Mill (just across the main road) houses a small collection of agricultural and cider making equipment and is open free of charge). Near the mill and the main road is a quaint dome shaped structure, this is a dipping well which was used to collect water.

Bossington church is clearly visible from a long distance as it is the only one that is still periodically painted white with a lime/tallow coat to protect it. It has a very old clock which strikes a bell, but has no exterior clock face. Inside the church is one of the finest waggon-roofs in England. At the corner of the churchyard is a sign pointing the way for those who wish to make the short excursion into the woods to Bury Castle.

Lynch Combe is an ideal picnic spot with a stream, trees to climb, and good views.

Refreshments   There are cafes in Bossington, Allerford and Selworthy; also nearby at Horner. The nearest inn is at Porlock.

Minehead and North Hill

Outline   Minehead Harbour ~ St. Michael's Church ~ Burgundy Chapel ~ North Hill Woodcombe ~ Church steps ~ Harbour.

Summary   The walk rises to the Church, passes through woods high above the sea to Burgundy Chapel before climbing over North Hill. The return is through the picturesque area at Church Steps.

Attractions   Minehead was a port in the 14th century. Today it is a pleasant seaside resort. Quay Town sits on the harbour and houses the R.N.L.I. lifeboat station and a 17th century fisherman's chapel. High Town has cottages of a local style with chimneys adjacent to the street and a small window in the lower part forming a look out. Cob cottages (with walls of loam, straw, and small stones stand along a steeply rising cobbled street. Low town contains all the modern development.

Francis Eales said of St. Michael's Church "Few of our churches are more strikingly situated". The tower has interesting carvings and inside is a 15th century font, a 17th century carved pulpit, 16th century screen and the quaint figure of Jack The Hammer. A stained glass window shows scenes in the Lord's life. Glass cases house rare books and an illuminated missal. You may hear the peal of 10 bells whilst walking.

Above the church there are fine views of the terminus of the West Somerset Railway line and the coast and there are lovely woods high above the sea. Look down here to see if there are any visible signs at low water of the submarine forest in which various forms of prehistoric life have been found.

The walks on North Hill were laid out by the Lord of the Manor and the woods are a delight in winter as well as summer due to the variety of evergreens including evergreen oaks, rhododendrons, cherry laurel, and some magnificent pines; a grand place for hide and seek.

At the National Trust's Greenaleigh Point property, a track lined with pennywort, cuckoo pint and lesser celandine remind the walker that they have left the artificial environment of the woods and started on the real Somerset coastline, although the actual Coast Path is inland from this path. A path on the right at Greenaleigh Farm offers a diversion down to the beach.

At Burgundy Chapel a sign points left to the steep hill, but the medieval chapel is hiding on the right.

continued on page 42

Route 8

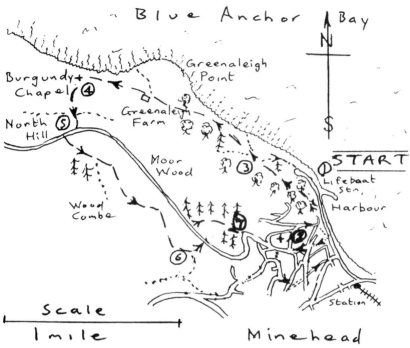

QUAY TOWN, MINEHEAD

Route 8
Minehead and North Hill
6 miles
(Shorter variations 2 and 4 miles)

START   *From the Lifeboat Station at Minehead Quay (G.R.970472).*

ROUTE

1. *Walk from the Lifeboat Station back towards the town to the sign indicating the start of the South West Path to Poole in Dorset. Turn right here up the steps, at the top of the steps (do not follow the coast path) follow Church Path ahead. This path bends right, then, where it ends, turn left into Saint Michael's Road, which runs straight and then turns right to the church.*

2. *At the church, Church Steps lies to the left, but you turn right, keeping the church on your left up Church Road, and then bearing right to join Beacon Road. Follow this road ahead and then bear left, following it until it enters the woods as a tarmac path, and the road itself turns sharply to the right and falls away. Follow the path for 200 yards.*

3. *The path splits into three; a tarmac path rises left and a path drops to the right but follow the middle path ahead, nearly level, all the way, to emerge from the woodland at the boundary of the National Trust Property of Greenaleigh Point. Pass to the right of Greenaleigh Farm, ignoring a path on the right leading to the shore. Keep straight ahead to the Burgundy Chapel.*

4. *At the chapel, turn left up the steep hill to join the coast path at the top, and then go straight ahead to an open piece of land used as a car park and on to the road.*

5. *Turn right on the road and after 100 yards turn left down a path into the combe swinging to the left. After a path branches right by a wall/bank remain on the main path down the combe for 150 yards then turn uphill. After 50 yards, turn right to follow a level path contouring around the shoulder of the hill.*

6. *At a small covered reservoir surrounded by a fence, Jim's Path joins from the left, a path drops to the right, but follow the path ahead to the road. Turn left up the road with the camping site on your right. 400 yards from the site entrance, turn right along a wide path into the pine trees. 50 yards into the wood turn right (signed "Higher Town") and follow the combe down to the road (600 yards after entering the wood there is an alternative path on the right for pedestrians, leading down to the road also, but avoiding the muddy bridle path).*

41

7. *Bear left on to the road, fork right down Moor Road. At the bottom, turn left to Church Steps, then turn right downhill to meet Middle Street. Bear left then right to The Holloway, turn left into Clanville Road. At the end of Clanville Road, take the footpath opposite, across Martlet Road, which leads down to the sea front. Turn left along the front to the Lifeboat Station.*

SHORTER VARIATIONS

i *At the end of Beacon Road (just before point 3) branch right down the coast path to return to the sea front by the harbour.*

ii *From Burgundy Chapel, return the way you came but after the farm, branch left in the woods and walk down to the sea front and Lifeboat Station.*

The open spaces of North Hill make a fine adventure area. A viewpoint above Woodcombe gives views south to the wooded flanks of Periton Hill and Hopcutt Common and in the distance the conical mound of Conygar Hill. Atop the hill is Conygar Tower, a folly built in 1775 overlooking Dunster.

Save a few exposures on your film until you reach the quaint houses at Church Town at the foot of Church Steps.

Refreshments There are several cafes and public houses in the town but none en-route.

DUNSTER CASTLE

Route 9

Dunster and Grabbist Hill

Outline   Dunster Car Park ~ Dovecote ~ Butter Cross ~ Grabbist Hill ~ Church ~ Yarn Market ~ Car Park.

Summary   The walk explores the interesting corners of Dunster and then rises to a spectacular viewpoint overlooking two ancient settlements.

Attractions   Dunster is a picturesque village with its 16th century yarn market surrounded by charming buildings, set with cobbled pavements dominated by the castle and overlooked by Conygar Tower. This walk takes you around the interesting back lanes and into the walled gardens of the village.

At the start there is the information centre of the Exmoor National Park. Priory Green is named after the former Benedictine Priory which stood here and the stone arches of the priory gates still stand over the road where you glimpse views of the church and castle. On the right is the restored Norman dovecote and on the left is the tythe barn and to the right of the barn is a large door and a small door. The former leads into a large walled garden beyond which is another door leading to another garden full of interesting plants. The small door from Priory Green leads into another heavenly garden with a well into which you can cast your wish and your coins.

The Butter Cross was originally in The Shambles in the market place but it now offers a convenient resting place with a view of Conygar Tower before starting the ascent to Grabbist Hill.

The escarpment of Grabbist Hill dominates the lovely vale of the River Avill. Beyond the river the wooded slopes rise up to the clear tops above the Deer Park where one can discern two ancient earthworks. The nearest is a circular camp of British origin. The distant Roman camp, known as Bat's Castle, had a double vallum of stones and a fosse. On your right, a depression in the hill is called The Giant's Chair where the giant sat to bathe his feet in the River Avill below. The surrounding woods are a great place for hide and seek. A soft mossy carpet covers the surface of this spectacular viewpoint from where a ridge leads steeply down through a lovely woodland.

When leaving the churchyard, if you have time, take a diversion to the right down the cobbled pavements of West Street which leads to Mill Lane and the old corn mill where you can watch corn being ground. If you

continued on page 46

43

Route 9

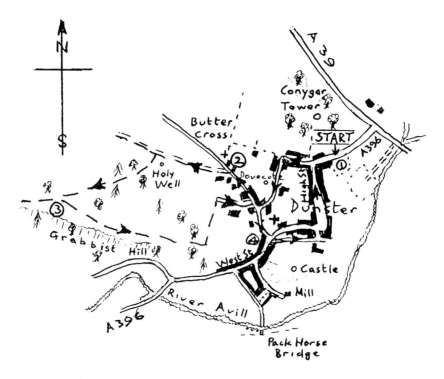

Route 9

Dunster and Grabbist Hill

3½ miles

(Shorter variation 2 miles)

START   *From the car park adjacent to the A396 at the northern end of Dunster.*

ROUTE

1. *From the car park walk towards the village along the A396 for 80 yards and take the right hand fork (out of High Street) into The Ball and then Priory Green. Bear left (this road is still Priory Green) where a public footpath leads ahead along a house drive to the Butter Cross. Diversions off the road (Priory Green) lead into the gardens on the left and to the Dovecote on the right, but at the end of Priory Green turn right into Saint Georges Street and note the path, left, which is the return route. Ascend Saint Georges Street (passing Hangers Way on the left, where another footpath leads up Conduit Lane to Grabbist Hill) to reach the Butter Cross on the right a few feet back from the road.*

2. *Return from the Butter Cross down the road to turn right into Conduit Lane as the lane climbs up towards Grabbist Hill. Pass the site of the Holy Well on your left then, 40 yards beyond the well, turn left into the woods. Follow the path as it bends to the right and rises, passing two paths which join from the left. Eventually the wood thins and open fields on the right give views to the sea. Just beyond here, where the path flattens out on nearing the summit, turn sharp left to reach the open hilltop overlooking the escarpment on your right.*

3. *Walk along the ridge heading South East towards Dunster and follow the ridge as it falls steeply. At the bottom, where the woodland ends, cross the path to leave the wood and walk with allotments on your left and the cemetery on the right. Turn right after the second cemetery site, then turn right into St. Georges Street to enter the lych gate to the church door. Turn right to reach the junction of Church Street and West Street.*

4. *Turn left into Church Street to reach High Street, turn left into High Street at the castle entrance. Follow High Street past the Yarn Market, and bear right to return to the car park.*

SHORTER VARIATION

From the Butter Cross, return down St. Georges Street to the Lych Gate and follow the church path to the right to point 4 and onward.

45

have both time and energy left, then make the steep but rewarding climb to the castle. There has been a castle on the site for 1000 years but the oldest part of the present structure is the 13th century gateway. It was a focal point in the civil war but peace now reigns at the top of the castle, approached through the tropical garden with luxuriant evergreens and blooms of mimosa and magnolia. When nearing the end of the walk in High Street, before dashing into one of the welcoming tea shops, closely examine the Yarn Market to find the hole in the roof supports made by a canon ball in the civil war; nearby stands the Dolls' Museum. As the route leaves High Street a narrow alley on the left leads to Conygar Tower if you want still further adventure.

Refreshments There is a wide choice of refreshments in the village.

DOVECOTE AT DUNSTER (Route 9)

46

Route 10

Wheddon Cross, Dunkery Gate, Dunkery Beacon

Outline Wheddon Cross ~ Raleigh Manor ~ Dunkery Gate ~ Dunkery Beacon ~ Dunkery Gate ~ Mansley Combe ~ Wheddon Cross.

Summary The walk passes through woodland before reaching the open moorland at Dunkery Gate for a taste of the wilder Exmoor. Here there is the option to reach the highest point on Exmoor, Dunkery Beacon, before dropping into a wild wooded combe for the return to Wheddon Cross.

Attractions While walking in the woods you may catch sight of red deer if you are quiet enough, or, more likely you will see the flash of their light coloured rump as they scurry away through the undergrowth. Dunkery Gate is on the edge of the open moor and is a good place for a picnic at the half way stage before returning or before tackling the optional extra pull up to the heights of Dunkery Beacon. The Beacon is covered in heather and is a splendid sight in late summer. The summit at 1700 feet above sea level affords a magnificent panorama and is a grand open space for kites although beware if mist is around - make sure you have a compass and know how to use it. The return is through very wild woodland where children with a sense of imagination can have a grand time. Undergrowth crowds in on the path which crosses several streams (waterproof boots are quite an asset here) before emerging from the woods to find a small bridge by a boggy area, which is a delightful spot to rest and count the variety of wild plants.

Refreshments At Wheddon Cross there is a tea shop/barbers shop (a unique combination?) and an inn, appropriately named the "Rest and Be Thankful".

Route 10

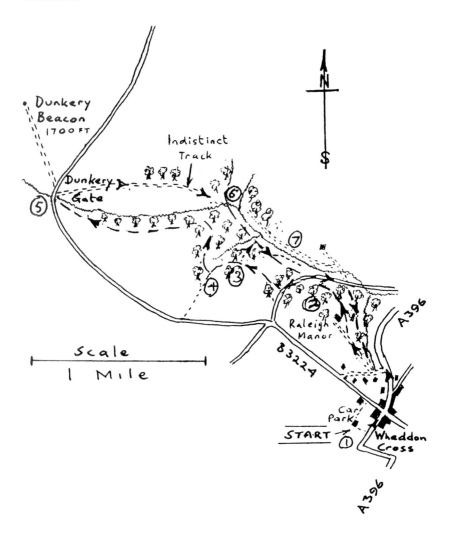

Route 10

Wheddon Cross, Dunkery Gate, Dunkery Beacon   6½ miles
(Shorter variation 5 miles)

START   *From the car park/toilets adjoining the "Rest and Be Thankful Inn" at Wheddon Cross (G.R.923388) at the junction of the A396 with the B3224.*

ROUTE

1. *Walk from the car park with the inn on your left and turn left on to the main road A396. Cross the road junction and continue to follow the main road as it bends left downhill until you reach a narrow tarmac lane which drops to the left (signposted bridlepath to Dunkery Gate). Follow this lane down towards the farm and, after it crosses the stream, bear right through the trees (ignoring left hand forks) to follow a tarmac drive leading to Raleigh Manor. Just before the gate into the grounds of the manor, a hedge branches off to the right. Follow this, keeping the hedge on your right to walk down into the wood. Continue to a tarmac lane.*

2. *Turn left up the tarmac lane and turn right after 100 yards through a gate into the wood. Follow this path through the conifers to emerge into a clearing, and then enter oak woodland at the far side of the clearing to follow a well defined path through the woods.*

3. *A path merges into your route from the right. Continue ahead, on fairly level ground.*

4. *Turn right here where the original route starts to climb between two banks running along either side. Follow this new route down and then fairly level until it reaches the top of the wood at a small gate. Do not use this gate but stay on the path which runs along the top of the valley just inside the wood. Pass out of the wood at the next gate and immediately re-enter at the next gate and follow the path at the top of the woodland until another small gate leads out of the wood. Follow the same direction to pass through two more gates and reach the road.*

5. *Turn right on to the road and over the small bridge. The second path on the left leading away from the road at 45° is the well worn path to Dunkery Beacon if you wish to make that excursion (1½ miles return). The track on the right hand side of the road is the return route to Wheddon Cross. Follow the track to the right through the gate and across open land until you cross a ditch and a line of beech trees. Here take the right hand path leading slightly downhill towards another line of beeches. Continuing in the same direction, pass these beeches on your left hand side and continue in the same direction for 50 yards. Then bear*

49

right downhill to a field gate. Pass through the gate and bear 45° left to follow the same direction as previously and walk downhill to find the well worn path in the bottom of the valley.

6. *Several streams converge here. Follow the stream down through the woods until you finally emerge with the stream on your left.*

7. *At the small bridge take the right fork to walk uphill to the road (point 2). Turn left down the road and then turn right along the path through the woods. Follow this path through the woods, with the valley on your left until you reach the tarmac drive along which you first came. Follow the drive up to the road and bear right to follow the road back to the car park.*

SHORTER VARIATION

At point 3 turn sharp right and follow the path down into the bottom of the valley to point 7.

TARR STEPS

Route 11

8 miles

(Shorter variation 2½ miles)

Tarr Steps, Withypool Hill, Withypool

Outline   Tarr Steps ~ Parsonage Down ~ Withypool Hill ~ Withypool ~ Tarr Steps.

Summary   The walk descends from the car park to Tarr Steps and then rises to Withypool Hill (1300 ft.) before dropping into the village of Winsford to follow the valley back to Tarr Steps.

Attractions   The car park itself is set in glorious scenery above the River Barle. Tarr Steps is a delightful spot, where the old packhorse bridge stands alongside a ford across the river. Children play at the waters edge whilst waiting for the occasional car or horse to venture across the ford. The bridge is a 17th century clapper bridge of gritstone and generally thought to be of mediaeval origin, but having been repaired several times due to flood damage.

Withypool Hill is a vast area of heather moor to play and explore; search very carefully and you can discover a stone circle hidden in the heather. Atop the hill are the remains of an ancient barrow. The return along the river is a delight for all the family. There are so many picnic spots that is difficult to choose. About ½ mile from Withypool, notice the stepping stones across the river. Beyond Hindspit Bridge notice the rocky outcrop which seems to have both horizontal and vertical layering and notice the debris trap, strung across the river like a Tarzan jungle bridge.

Refreshments   The Royal Oak at Withypool has a bar and a restaurant. From April to October Tarr Farm at Tarr Steps provides refreshments. The nearest refreshments otherwise are at Dulverton and Exford.

Route 11

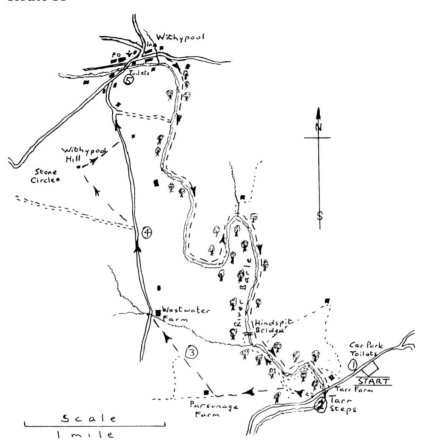

Route 11

Tarr Steps, Withypool Hill, Withypool   8 miles
(Shorter variation 2½ miles)

START *From the car park/toilets above the East bank of the River Barle. (G.R.873325), this is signposted off the B3223 North of Dulverton.*

ROUTE

1. *Walk downhill from the car park along the lane to the river.*
2. *Cross the clapper bridge and follow the track which forks to the right about 50 yards from the river. Shortly a track branches off left into the hotel. Follow the main track as it climbs and then swings right, leaving the woodland on the left. Where the track passes through a hedge/bank turn left to climb up the field, keeping the hedge on your left. At the top, pass through the gate and walk straight ahead keeping the hedge on your left. Turn right at Parsonage Farm to keep the farm on your left, and walk uphill, keeping the hedge on your left. At the top of the hill, pass through the gate in this hedge to maintain the same direction, but with the hedge now on the right, to reach a stile.*
3. *At the stile maintain the same direction (although a sign offers a diversion left to Withypool Hill via an old barrow) walking downhill to meet the road. Turn right, to follow it for about ½ mile to a cattle grid.*
4. *The cattle grid is at the edge of the open moor, and to the left can be seen the summit of Withypool Hill. Walk to the top of the hill and then turn right to regain the road which drops down into Withypool.*
5. *Cross the bridge and bear right, passing the toilets on the right and the Royal Oak on the left. Cross a small stream and follow the road uphill to a stile on the right. Cross the stile and follow the path left, above the river, until it drops to river level. Follow the river bank back to Tarr Steps, and there turn left to return to the car park.*

SHORTER VARIATION

At point 2 cross the bridge and follow the river to the right. Cross the river at the first bridge (Hindspit Bridge) and turn right to return to Tarr Steps.

DULVERTON HOUSE

Route 12

Dulverton and Court Down

Outline   Dulverton (Exmoor House) ~ Town Hall ~ Court Down ~ Marsh Bridge ~ Exmoor House.

Summary   Starting from the river and passing the town centre, the walk rises to reach the open hilltop of Court Down before descending to the charming valley of the River Barle to return to Dulverton.

Attractions   Dulverton is a gem set on the banks of the River Barle at the edge of the National Park, with wooded slopes rising above. The Saxons named it The Secret Place and here the legendary James Ridd first saw Lorna Doone. Exmoor National Park headquarters are beside the river and there is an adjoining car park, picnic area, and toilets where the walk starts. Behind the house is Dulverton Art Gallery.

Notice the mark on the wall on the right of the main street which indicates the height of the flood water here on the night of the Lynmouth flood disaster in August 1952, when a huge cloudburst caused a massive discharge of water to descend from Exmoor; could it happen again?

The Town Hall has a unique frontage with steps rising over an arch to the canopied entrance to the main hall (picture the crinolines floating up to the ball in the days of Lorna Doone). The other buildings crowd around to form a delightful composition.

The lane rising up to Court Down is lined with a varied array of wild plants including hart's tongue, pennywort and lesser celandine. At one point it is bounded by beech hedges, which are a typical feature of the Exmoor scene, while the open top of Court Down affords a fantastic panoramic view.

Marsh Bridge is a spot to rest on the benches in a picturesque setting and watch the river glide by, or have some waterside fun. Beyond the bridge the lane is lined on the left with a wide variety of flora while on the right, rhododendrons display their purple summer mantle. Here, I saw three red deer in flight from the hunt while a heron flew gracefully overhead. At Kennels Farm a notice on a gate warns of a forty shillings fine for leaving the gate open, and railway buffs may puzzle over the railway's initials on the notice "GS&WR" (Clue - it was British but over the water).

The woods on the final stage of the walk have rhododendrons in one part and holly in another, to give plenty of cover for hide and seek while

continued on page 58

55

Route 12

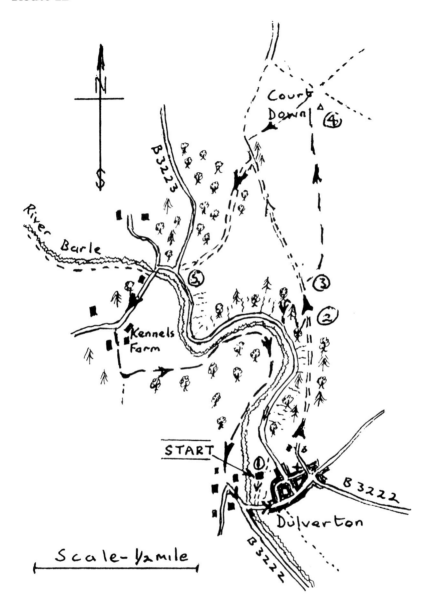

N S

B3223

River Barle

Court Down ④

⑤

③

②

Kennels Farm

START ①

Dulverton

B3222

B3222

Scale - ½ mile

56

Route 12

Dulverton and Court Down

5 miles

(Shorter variations 3 or 4 miles)

START *At the car park adjacent to the river and the Exmoor National Park Information Centre off the B3222 in Dulverton. (G.R.913279).*

ROUTE

1. *Walk back from the car park towards the bridge and turn left into the main street. Take the left fork and pass the Town Hall, heading towards the church. Walk up the narrow alley with the church on your left then turn left up the lane. Follow the lane as it swings right and continues to rise.*

2. *After climbing along the lane for approximately 600 yards, you reach point 2 just beyond a group of pine trees on the left. Here, a hedge of evergreens (laurel and rhododendrons) on the right mark the point where a path (look carefully in the wood to find the start) leaves our route to the left and forms the short route. However, follow the lane for the main route.*

3. *100 yards beyond point 2 the woodland is left behind, and there are fields on both sides. Turn through the gate on the right and immediately bear left uphill towards a line of trees and a hedge. Pass through the line of trees and, a few yards further, turn approximately 45° to the left to pass through the gate in the hedge and follow a hedge on your left. You should now be walking nearly parallel to the lane which you have just left. Follow the hedge on your left (walking in a shallow depression) for approximately 600 yards, passing over a drive and through a copse, then an open field, to reach a third gate. Pass through this gate on to the open hilltop and reach the Ordnance Survey pillar at the summit of Court Down.*

4. *To return from the summit, turn round to face the way from which you came and walk forwards but towards the hedge on your right to pass through a gate in the corner of the field. Bear left to follow the hedge on your left. After 300 yards bear left on to a track and through a gate into a lane. Fork right down a wide path to Marsh Bridge (ignore the left fork half way down the hill).*

5. *Cross the road, turn right, then left over the river bridge, and follow the road to the next bend (at Kennels Farm). Go through the gate on the left and pass the farm to enter woodland. Follow the path as it bends left (ignore the right turn) and follow the river valley until it reaches a road.*

Follow the road downhill and turn left over the bridge and left into the car park.

SHORTER VARIATIONS

i *At point 2 turn left into the woods and follow the path as it traverses the wooded hillside winding down to the road. At the road, turn left. When the river leaves the road, continue to follow the narrower mill stream as it first follows the road, then flows behind the row of cottages, to return to the car park.*

ii *At point 3 carry straight on up the lane for nearly ½ mile to join the main route (just before the lane opens out on to the open hill between points 4 and 5) and turn sharp left down the wide path to Marsh Bridge. Continue as from 5.*

---

the path dips down to the river offering delightful waterside playspots. If anyone has any energy left when crossing the final bridge then walk downstream to the Trim Park Circuit.

WIMBLEBALL RESERVOIR

Route 13 5½ miles

Haddon Hill and Wimbleball Reservoir

Outline   Haddon Hill ~ Bury ~ Hartford Bottom ~ Wimbleball Dam ~ Haddon Hill.

Summary   The walk starts at the car park toilets and picnic area above Wimbleball Reservoir. It passes through a conifer plantation and drops downhill to Bury where it passes the ford and follows the river in Hartford Bottom. The walk climbs to the dam and then up the hill to finish.

Attractions   Haddon Hill stands 355 metres above sea level overlooking the Wimbleball Reservoir. Picnic areas, car park, toilets and a grand view (if you are not in low cloud) combine to make it a good start to the walk, which passes through a plantation of pine, spruce, and hemlock, then through oak woodland. The bridleway to Bury is lined with large crops of pennywort and primroses.

At Bury there is a delightful ford flanked by a picturesque footbridge where you can play Pooh Sticks and watch the horses and cars splash through the ford. The banks of the lane to the ford are covered in wild plants including wild strawberries, wood sorrel, cuckoo pint, pennywort and primroses.

Along the river in the woodland of Hartford Bottom are delightful picnic spots. Notice the gauging station with a depth indicator to monitor river flows. At Hartford the trout farm takes visitors by appointment.

At the approach to the dam a sign warns riders that a stallion runs with the Exmoor herd. The ponies have roamed the moor for thousands of years and have adapted to the severe weather. It is a very pure breed with a jaw similar to pre-historic animals and the Park Authority now manage two herds of ponies.

You will see huge buttresses on the large dam, the weight of which provides the stability to resist the overturning pressure of the water. A walk across the dam brings you to the spillway where water cascades down the dam in times of storm to prevent it flooding over the top of the dam. The water flows down a series of steps to absorb the energy rather than let the water rush to the bottom and damage the base of the dam. On the right is the take-off tower inside which are a series of valves to extract water at various levels. A diversion beyond the dam through pleasant woodland leads to the recreation area and the water sports centre.

The hill between the dam and the car park is the place to release any excess energy, play hide and seek or take a picnic.

continued on page 62

Route 13

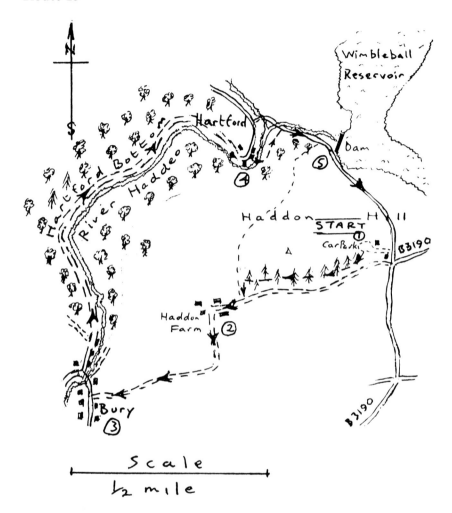

Route 13

Haddon Hill and Wimbleball Reservoir   5½ miles

START *From the car park/toilets at the South end of Wimbleball Reservoir (G.R.969286). Haddon Hill is signposted off the B3190 Bampton-Watchet road.*

ROUTE

1. *At the end of the car park away from where you entered, walk towards the fence around the conifer plantation and follow it to the right for a few yards i.e. towards the reservoir, then turn left to follow it for a few more yards to turn left through a wide gate on to the forest track through the conifers. Follow this wide path as it swings right and then runs fairly straight (ignore any turns left or right). After ½ mile it passes through a wide gate to join another wide path and continues in the same direction. The path enters deciduous woodland and turns right to a sheep fold on the edge of the wood. Just before the sheep fold, turn left downhill through the deciduous wood, keeping a hedge on your right, to meet a farm track. Turn right on to the track to Haddon Farm.*

2. *After passing the farmhouse at Haddon Farm, turn left down the lane between high banks. Follow the lane as it swings right and, ignoring any branches left or right, follow it down to Bury.*

3. *Turn right on to the tarmac road at Bury, cross the bridge over the river, and turn right into the narrow lane. Ignore the left fork where the lane rises uphill and follow the path along the valley to Hartford.*

4. *At Hartford a signpost points ahead to the dam via the houses. Following this sign, walk ahead through the garden gate into Hartford Mill and swing left to the far boundary of the garden, then turn right to the river, left to the bridge. Cross the bridge and turn left to follow the river to the concrete road. Turn right, pass through the gate, and ignoring the left forks, climb up the road to the dam.*

5. *Follow the road uphill beyond the dam (unless you wish to walk across the dam to the recreation area). After ½ mile, just before the road enters a woodland, turn right along the path to the car park.*

Refreshments There are no refreshment places en-route. Refreshments are available at the recreation area information office and there is a tea room at Brompton Regis. Dulverton and Bampton have cafes and public houses.

CROWCOMBE STATION

Crowcombe and Triscombe Stone

Outline   Crowcombe ~ Crowcombe Park Gate ~ Triscombe Stone ~ Triscombe ~ Crowcombe.

Summary   The walk passes along the village street at Crowcombe and then rises to the summit of the Quantocks, running along the ridge to Triscombe Stone from where it drops through Triscombe Combe and returns to Crowcombe via Triscombe village.

Attractions   Crowcombe is a small village at the western foot of the Quantocks with little more than a church, a public house, and a shop. The church is opposite the car park and must be visited, either before or after the walk. My impression of the outside of the church was that a large church had been shrunk to form a smaller one as so much stone carving had been designed into a relatively small area of wall and windows. Inside, the 16th century pews have superb carvings on the bench ends and the font is beautifully sculptured. In 1725 the spire was damaged by lightning and the top piece now rests in the churchyard. Adjacent to the car park is the 15th century Church House, very well preserved and still used by the Parish. Adjoining this is the pound in which straying animals were kept until their owners paid a fine for their release. The village had a market and a fair dating from the 13th century and after leaving the Church House, you will see the original market cross on the right, where people sat to sell their wares.

    After leaving the village you soon reach the open hilltop at Crowcombe Park Gate, an ideal spot to fly your kite, picnic, or admire the views from different points along the ridge.

    As you descend Triscombe Combe, there are plenty of places for a game of hide and seek before reaching the picturesque Blue Ball Inn at Triscombe with its lovely thatched roof.

Refreshments   There are public houses in Crowcombe and Triscombe.

    At Timberscombe, 4 miles East of Triscombe there is a cafe/gift shop (G.R.208329).

    In the village of West Bagborough there is a restaurant/pottery.

    Stable Cottage at Triscombe (G.R.152351) serves refreshments and has a display of pictures and horse tack.

E   63

Route 14

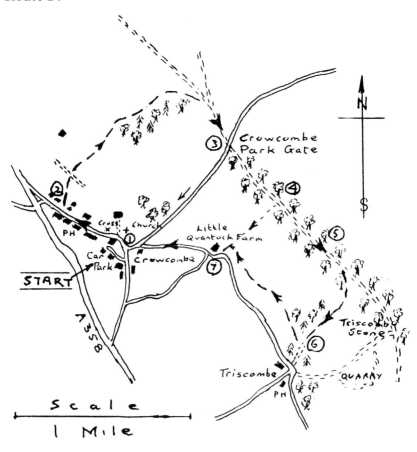

START

A358

Scale
1 Mile

Route 14

Crowcombe and Triscombe Stone

5 miles

(Shorter variation 3½ miles)

START   *From the car park opposite the church at Crowcombe (G.R.140367).*

ROUTE

1. *From the car park, go towards the church and turn left to walk along the road, passing Church House on your left, the church and the market on the right. 250 yards beyond the public house turn right up the steps which are adjacent to a terrace of modern houses.*

2. *Above the steps follow the path straight ahead, cross a broad track, keep the same direction (2 posts mark the path) and head for the tall pine trees in the woodland ahead. Follow the broad path along the side of this mixed woodland, with the wood on your right. As the wood ends on your right, you meet a beech hedge on the left; pass through the hedge at the gate and bear right along the path which runs just above the beech hedge, which now forms the boundary of the woodland. Cross the fence line to join the broad path, which continues to run parallel to the hedge, to reach the tarmac road (at Crowcombe Park Gate).*

3. *Cross the road and walk along the ridgeway track lined with beech trees for ½ mile to reach point 4.*

4. *The only feature to demark this point on the ridgeway path is the twin electricity line which comes up Little Quantock Combe on the right, crosses the path, and feeds to a farm on the left. A field gate on the right leads down the combe which is short variation (ii). The route continues along the ridge for another ¼ mile to enter the National Trust property "Great Hill and Marrow Hill" at point 5.*

5. *Do not follow the ridge path any further (ahead lies Triscombe Stone) but bear right at approximately 30 degrees along the open hill (Great Hill). You are now heading towards Triscombe Combe (no clear path is visible) but as you head away from the ridgeway you will soon find the combe coming into view ahead, with a group of beech, larch and Douglas fir lining the right hand edge of the combe below. Head for these trees and turn right down the combe. Follow the path in the bottom of the combe for ¼ mile to where the open land on your left becomes densely wooded.*

6. *At this wooded patch, turn sharp right uphill towards a wood of pine and spruce, and follow the path with the conifers on your right and a field boundary hedge on the left. Follow this path for ½ mile as it*

emerges from the wood, runs level for a little further, swings downhill to the left, then bears right to run (very indistinct here) alongside a row of conifer and old beech trees to reach Little Quantock Combe.

7. *Turn left down this combe to walk along the track through Little Quantock Farm and ahead down the lane. Swing right after the farm, ignore the left turn, and follow the lane to Crowcombe.*

SHORTER VARIATIONS

i *On reaching the tarmac road at Crowcombe Park Gate, Point 3, turn right and follow the road down to Crowcombe.*

ii *Half a mile beyond the road, i.e. at point 4, turn right off the ridgeway down Little Quantock Combe to point 7. Continue as for 7 above.*

HILL FORT, DOWSBOROUGH

Route 15

Nether Stowey and Crowcombe Park Gate

Outline   Nether Stowey ~ Stowey Castle ~ Walfords Gibbet ~ Five Lords ~ Dowsborough Fort ~ Crowcombe Park Gate ~ Rams Combe ~ Over Stowey ~ Nether Stowey.

Summary   A magnificent ramble passing two ancient fortifications, ascending through ancient oak woodland, emerging on to the summit ridge of the Quantocks, and descending through a coniferous combe.

Attractions   All the best poets can be found in all the best areas, and Nether Stowey is no exception, with its wooded combes, clear hill tops, and a coastal plain sheltered from the prevailing south west weather. Wordsworth had a house here which is now a hotel and Coleridge's house is now owned by the National Trust. This is where Coleridge wrote 'The Ancient Mariner' and the first part of 'Christobel'.

A stream runs down Castle Street and little bridges lead to the houses. Stowey Court (adjoining the church) has a grand 18th century gazebo. Shortly after leaving the car park and ascending Castle Street, on the right hand side is a striking statue set in the garden wall of Ivy Cottage. Despite first impressions to the contrary, the lady and her dog are quite recent in origin. At the crest of the narrow lane, on the right is the entrance to the remains of Stowey Castle, commanding magnificent views. The lane then falls and where it crosses a stream, on the right is a dipping well, a charming little structure.

The route rises up Bin Combe through ancient oak woodland with a wide variety of flora and fauna. The uphill leg of the route contrasts strongly with the downhill return through the conifers of Rams Combe. The old oaks are 'designed' for climbing. You will notice how some holly bushes have been grazed into low domed shapes.

Danesborough Camp (on top of Dowsborough) is a prehistoric earthwork. It is overgrown by oaks but it is oval in shape and the path passes through the cross section of the defences as it leaves, giving a clear view of its profile. Holford Combe has a delightful picnic spot beside the stepping stones, catching the sun, yet protected on all sides from the wind. On the ridge at Crowcombe Park Gate you will be tempted to roam along the tops to take your fill of the panorama. It is a fine place for kites and picnics.

The descent through the conifers of Rams Combe passes the Forestry Commission camp and picnic site which has barbecue and play

continued on page 70

Route 15

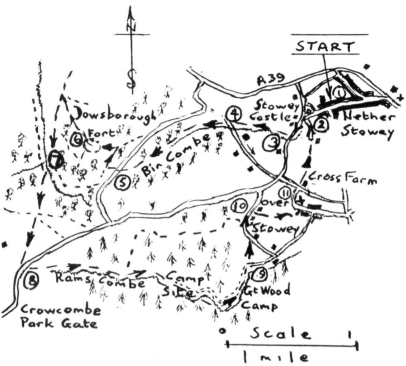

EAST QUANTOXHEAD

68

Route 15

Nether Stowey and Crowcombe Park Gate   8 miles

(Shorter variation 2½ miles)

START   *At the car park of the Library/Quantock Hills information centre, Castle Street, Nether Stowey. (G.R.191399).*

ROUTE

1. *Turn uphill from the car park into Castle Street and follow this road as it becomes a narrow lane (do not take the right fork at Butchers Lane).*

2. *Notice Hockpitts Lane on the left, which is the return route. Turn left at the next junction, and continue for a few yards.*

3. *Fork right along the broad path with the stream on your left. Cross the stile into the field to walk above the stream then, at the copse, cross the stile to the left down to stream level.*

4. *Cross the tarmac road, follow the wide path ahead to pass through the gate into the wood. Follow the path in the bottom of this combe as it rises through the oak woodland until it meets a road.*

5. *Across the road a path rises through the wood to the left (ignore any others). Take this left path and, after 60 yards, take the first right fork. This leads through a gap in a stone wall/hedge bank 200 yards from the road, to meet a wide path. Turn right to follow this path uphill with the bank on your right at first. Ignore the left hand fork and continue to climb uphill to a crossing of another wide path. Turn left on to the other path, rising to the summit of Dowsborough and the hill fort.*

6. *Turn right where a broad path cuts through the ramparts of the old hill fort and descend the hill for 300 yards, where a broad path joins from the right. Turn left here along a narrow path leading towards the combe. Follow the path as it bends to the left, enters the oak woodland and drops into the combe.*

7. *Looking across the stepping stones you will notice a broad path rising through the wood to the left, follow this. You emerge from the woodland after 400 yards and continue to rise across open heathland. Cross the wide track (where the gradient eases) and follow the path to the site of the pond and an ancient cairn on your left. Ignore the right fork at the pond and follow the path ahead (heading for a lonesome tree on the horizon). As you sight the road at Crowcombe Park Gate, notice the combe to the left which is the return route; a grassy path leads towards it.*

8. *From Crowcombe Park Gate, after exploring the summit, head East along the grassy path which you espied as you arrived. Follow this down into the conifers and along the forestry road down through Rams Combe, passing the camp/picnic site on your right.*

9. *At Great Wood Camp take the narrow path which forks left off the forest road (slightly overgrown). Emerge from the wood, cross the road and follow the path ahead to a gate. Enter the field and follow the path as it rises and bends to the left. Join the lane and carry straight ahead then round the right hand bend into the hamlet, which is the upper part of Over Stowey.*

10. *On the right is a field gate with a stone stile, and another gate just beyond. Cross the stile and the second gate and bear left to follow the hedge on your right down towards the churchyard. At the end of the hedge, turn right through the hedge and immediately left to a small gate and on to a drive to the church.*

11. *Turn left at Over Stowey Church and follow the road to a 'T' junction. Take the stile ahead into the field. Keep straight ahead, with the hedge on your left, to the next stile, and ahead again (with the hedge on your left) down to a gate. Follow the path, then the tarmac road to the road junction (point 2), where you turn right to return to the car park.*

SHORTER VARIATION

Turn left at Point 4 and follow the lane to the 'T' junction (point 11) and turn left over the stile.

---

areas. Over Stowey affords fine views of the Somerset Levels and distant Mendips. On the wall inside Over Stowey church is a plan showing the stages of its construction from the 14th century onwards. Another viewpoint is reached at Cross Farm with sight of the Welsh coast and the island of Steep Holm.

Refreshments Teas etc. may be obtained at the farm shop adjacent to the church on the main road A39. There are several public houses in Nether Stowey and two cafés.

Kilve — Lilstock — East Quantoxhead

Outline Kilve sea front car park ~ Kilton ~ Lilstock old harbour ~ Cliff path ~ Kilve beach ~ East Quantoxhead ~ Kilve car park.

Summary An interesting walk through fields, along the cliff top and visiting churches, a duck pond, and an old oil distillation plant with fossil hunting on the beach.

Attractions On the journey down to the Exmoor area, Kilve often presents the first opportunity to have a break at the sea edge, as resorts along the Bristol Channel passed earlier on the journey see little of the sea, except at high tide. It presents an opportunity to stand on the cliff top, look inland and see the backdrop of the Quantocks where the tree clad slopes rise quickly up from the South side of the A39 main road, reaching up along the wooded combes towards the open ridge line.

The veneer of agricultural land between the cliff and the hills covers shale beds up to 1000 feet deep and extending up to 2 miles inland. In 1916 these were found to be rich in oil and the Shaline Company was formed to exploit the oil. At the end of the car park is the retort house which was used to extract the oil.

The ivy clad ruins which you pass on leaving the car park are of Kilve Chantry, reputedly a smuggler's den before it was destroyed by fire. Nearby is a delightful duck pond, at the road junction.

From the high point on the route you can see the distant Hinkley Point nuclear power station, while below lies Kilton church. From Kilton your way is lined with hedges full of reeds and iris leading to Saint Andrew's church, a delightful building which looks as though it has just fallen off the icing of a cake.

At the entrance to Lilstock beach notice the ammonite in the gate pillar. There are plenty of stones to throw in the sea at Lilstock and the shale strata provides plenty of flat stones for skimming.

A search in the undergrowth at Lilstock reveals the remains of the old harbour together with a more recent structure, a second world war pill box. The harbour forms a sheltered picnic and play area. Atop the sea wall is a growth of Tamarix Callica, a feathery shrub which can grow up to 30 feet high and is covered with pink and white flowers from July to September. The sea wall is reinforced here with gabions (steel mesh cages filled with stone) to prevent the sea breaking through.

continued on page 72

Route 16

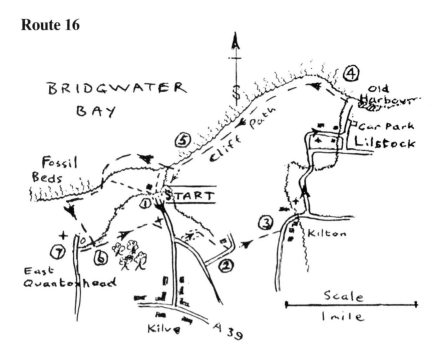

Before crossing the stile at the end of the sea wall, step on to the beach and look at the exposed strata forming the cliffs; this will help to understand the rock layers on the beach lying one on top of the other which look at low tide like old pavements superimposed one on the other.

A careful study of Kilve beach will reveal huge fossils, probably the biggest ammonites you are likely to find anywhere. William Wordsworth admired Kilve's delightful shore.

East Quantoxhead is a charming spot untouched by time with its Jacobean Court House next to Saint Mary's church and its duck pond, and thatched cottages. Don't forget to bring something for the ducks.

On your holiday route you may have noticed the distinctive shape of Glastonbury Tor on the Somerset Levels; now go into Kilve church and find the colourful window which depicts the story of Joseph of Arimathea who landed at Glastonbury and put his staff in the ground, to grow into the Holy Thorn.

Refreshments Various cafes and inns are available on the main A39 road but there are none on the immediate route of the walk.

Route 16

Kilve, Lilstock, East Quantoxhead

8½ miles

(Shorter variation 6 miles)

START *From the beach car park at Kilve; this is ¾ mile north of Kilve village, which lies on the A39 road (G.R.145444).*

ROUTE

1. *Start by walking back up the lane along which you have just driven. Turn left at the pond and left again up a narrow track. Pass through a gate into a field and immediately turn right over a stream and over a stile, then walk along the field with a copse of oak and a stream on the left. Cross two more stiles and bear to the left, keeping close to the copse. At the end of the copse cross the stile on your right and head for the right hand side of the new house ahead.*

2. *Turn left at the house on to the road and walk up to and through the gate ahead. Keeping the hedge on your right climb uphill to the high point and then straight ahead downhill, through the gate. Swing left, then right and through the gate to turn left on to the road.*

3. *Walk along the road through the hamlet of Kilton then turn left to pass the church on your left. Follow the lane down to a "Z" bend and then uphill to pass the tiny church of St. Andrew on your right, after which you follow the lane as it bends to the right. Turn left at the next "T" junction to pass through Lilstock car park and reach the sea wall with the old harbour on your right.*

4. *Turn left at the sea wall and follow the cliff top.*

5. *Stay on the path nearest the cliff top at Kilve. Descend to the beach if you wish to hunt for fossils before resuming the walk along the cliff top westwards, to the point where the path turns left to run inland. Follow this path towards East Quantoxhead.*

6. *600 yards from the cliffs, cross the stream to reach a 'T' junction of paths, turn right. (The path on your left will later be the return route).*

7. *On reaching the village pond at East Quantoxhead turn right through the car park to reach the church. After inspecting the church retrace your steps to point 6. Cross the fields straight ahead until you pass through the small gate in the wall of Kilve churchyard. After crossing the churchyard turn left at the road and return to the car park.*

SHORTER VARIATION

At point 5, rather than joining the beach, keep to the left hand path with the cricket field on your left, and go through the scrubby woodland to return to the car park.

Appendices

ROUTES IN ORDER OF DIFFICULTY

Starting with the easiest:

Route 5 - *Simonsbath and Cow Castle (Variation 1) — 1 mile*
Route 9 - *Dunster and Grabbist Hill (Variation 1) — 2 miles*
Route 2 - *Hunters Inn and Heddons Mouth Cleave (Variation 1) — 2 miles*
Route 11 - *Tarr Steps, Withypool Hill, Withypool (Variation 1) —2½ miles*
Route 6 - *Porlock, Bossington, Porlock Weir (Variation 1) — 3 miles*
Route 7 - *Bossington, Selworthy, Bossington Hill (Variation 1) —4 miles*
Route 1 - *Combe Martin and Great Hangman (Variation 1) — 3 miles*
Route 3 - *Lynton and Valley of the Rocks (Variation 1) — 2½ miles*
Route 8 - *Minehead and North Hill (Variation 1) — 2 miles*
Route 4 - *Malmsmead, Oare Church, Lorna Doone Valley (Variation 1) — 3 miles*
Route 16 - *Kilve, Lilstock, East Quantoxhead (Variation 1) — 6 miles*
Route 15 - *Nether Stowey and Crowcombe Park Gate (Variation 1) —2½ miles*
Route 3 - *Lynton, Valley of the Rocks — 3¾ miles*
Route 14 - *Crowcombe and Triscombe Stone (Variation 1) — 3½ miles*
Route 12 - *Dulverton and Court Down (Variation 1) — 3 miles*
Route 9 - *Dunster and Grabbist Hill — 3½ miles*
Route 8 - *Minehead and North Hill (Variation 2) — 4 miles*
Route 2 - *Hunters Inn and Heddons Mouth Cleave — 4 miles*
Route 6 - *Porlock, Bossington, Porlock Weir — 6 miles*
Route 7 - *Bossington, Selworthy, Bossington Hill — 6 miles*
Route 12 - *Dulverton and Court Down (Variation 2) — 4 miles*
Route 12 - *Dulverton and Court Down — 5 miles*
Route 10 - *Wheddon Cross, Dunkery Gate, Dunkery Beacon (Variation 1) — 5 miles*
Route 14 - *Crowcombe and Triscombe Stone — 5 miles*
Route 13 - *Haddon Hill and Wimbleball Reservoir — 5½ miles*
Route 8 - *Minehead and North Hill — 6 miles*
Route 10 - *Wheddon Cross, Dunkery Gate, Dunkery Beacon — 6½ miles*
Route 1 - *Combe Martin and Great Hangman — 6½ miles*
Route 16 - *Kilve, Lilstock, East Quantoxhead — 8½ miles*
Route 4 - *Malmsmead, Oare Church, Lorna Doone Valley — 7 miles*
Route 5 - *Simonsbath and Cow Castle — 7 miles*
Route 15 - *Nether Stowey and Crowcombe Park Gate — 8 miles*
Route 11 - *Tarr Steps, Withypool Hill, Withypool — 8 miles*

NATIONAL TRUST PROPERTIES

The National Trust owns and protects many properties in the Exmoor and Quantocks area, many of these walks pass over their land; I hope you enjoy using their facilities and give them your support financially, or in working parties or otherwise. The Holnicote Estate of 12400 acres includes Dunkery and Selworthy Beacons and the lovely model village of Selworthy and much of the coast is under their protection. They have an Information Centre and lovely tea room at Watersmeet House, set at the confluence of the East Lyn and Hoar Oak Water. Lundy Island is leased by the Trust to the Landmark Trust and boat trips are available from Bideford.

Fyne Court is leased to the Somerset Trust for Nature Conservation who have laid out several walks and nature trails open all the year.

Some of the other main properties are listed below:-

Dunster Castle and garden. Open April to end of September daily except Fri. and Sat. In June, July and Aug. the grounds are open on Fri. and Sat. also. The castle dates from the 13th century and the terraced gardens are planted with rare shrubs.

Dunster Water Mill. Open April to end of October, daily except Sat.; also open Sat. in July and August. A working mill, run and maintained by private funds.

Arlington Court near Barnstaple (signed off the A39). House and gardens open April to end October daily except Sat. Also open Sat. at Bank Holiday weekends.

Knightshayes Court and Gardens, Bolham, Tiverton. Open April to end October daily (house closed on Fridays). A richly decorated interior and magnificent garden.

Coleridge Cottage, in the village of Nether Stowey, West of Bridgwater, off the A39. Open April to end of September. Coleridge's home where he wrote "The Ancient Mariner".

Full details of National Trust properties may be obtained from their area offices at Stourton, Wiltshire (0747 840224) for Somerset, or from Killerton House, Broadclyst near Exeter (0392 881691) for Devon.

MUSEUMS AND PLACES OF ARCHITECTURAL OR HISTORIC INTEREST

Allerford Rural Life Museum. In Allerford village, just off the A39 near Porlock. Easter to October, Mon. to Sat. 10.30 to 12.30 and 14.00 till 16.30. Rural life museum with Victorian kitchen, craft workers' tools, old school room.

Barford Park, Enmore. 4 miles West of Bridgwater. May to September, Wed., Thur. and Bank Holiday weekends; otherwise by appointment.

Chambercombe Manor, Chambercombe Road, Ilfracombe. Easter Sunday to end Sept. Mon. to Fri. 10.30 till 17.00. Sun. 14.00 till 17.30. Dates from 11th century. Period furniture, grounds in wooded valley with gardens.

Cleeve Abbey, Washford. Just South of the A39. Good Friday or April 1st to 30th September daily 10.00 till 18.00. Rest of year, Tue. to Sun. 10.00 till 16.00. Cistercian building with complete set of cloisters, magnificent hall roof.

Dunster Water Mill, Mill Lane, Dunster. April to October daily, 11.00 till 17.00. Every day in August, September. Built in 1680 alongside River Avill. See flour ground and bagged.

Gaulden Manor, Lydeard Saint Lawrence, 7 miles West of Taunton. April to June, Sundays and Thursdays; July to early September, Sundays, Wednesdays, Thursdays; also Easter Sun. and Mon; 14.00 till 17.30. Also parties by appointment.

Hallsway Manor, near Crowcombe. Normally used for folk dancing courses etc., but arrangements can be made to visit. Telephone 09848 274.

Hestercombe Gardens, Cheddon Fitzpaine, 4 miles North of Taunton. All year Monday to Friday 9.00 till 17.00; also May to September, Saturday and Sunday 14.00 till 17.00. Beautifully restored Edwardian garden.

Lyn and Exmoor Museum, Queen Street, Lynton. Easter to end of September, Mon. to Sat. 9.00 till 17.00. Sundays 14.00 till 17.00. Exhibits of local interest.

Lynmouth Flood Memorial Hall, Riverside Road, Lynmouth. Easter to September, daily. Selection of photographs and flood memorabilia.

Museum of North Devon, The Square, Barnstaple. All year, Tue. to Sat. 10.00 till 16.30. Incorporates the Royal Devon Yeomanry Museum. Natural science, archeology, fine arts.

Orchard Mill Museum, Williton. Just South of the A39. March 1st to 31st December 10.00 till 18.00 (closed Mondays but open Bank Holiday Mondays). Agricultural implements and Victorian and Edwardian bygones, craft shop.

Saint Anne's Chapel and Old Grammar School Museum, St. Peters Churchyard, Barnstaple. June to October Mon. to Sat. 10.00 til 13.00 and 14.00 till 16.30 (closed Wed. afternoons). 14th century chapel, 17th century schoolroom, museum of schooling.

Tarr Steps Clapper Bridge. South West of the B3223 between Dulverton and Exford. Very ancient bridge, reconstructed and in daily use.

Tiverton Castle, Tiverton town centre. Mid April to end of September, Sunday to Thursday 14.30 till 17.30. Major West Country castle, civil war armoury, clock collection.

Tiverton Museum, Tiverton town centre. February to December, Monday to Saturday 10.30 till 16.30. Various exhibitions, galleries and photographs. Donations requested.

Watchet Market House Museum. Adjoining the quay. Artifacts relating to the history of the sea port. Staffed by volunteers.

West Somerset Railway, Washford Station, Museum. On the A39 road between Bridgwater and Minehead. Easter to end October, Sun. and Bank Holidays 11.00 till 17.00. Also daily late July to end October. (Also G.W.R. Museum, Blue Anchor Station on summer Sundays).

OTHER ATTRACTIONS

Animal Magic, Bossington. East of the A39 near Porlock. Mid March to end September 10.30 till 16.30 (closed on Sundays). Thatched farm dating from Saxon times, animal rides, picnic area.

Brass Rubbing and Hobbycraft Centre, Lynmouth. Adjacent Watersmeet Road car park. March to September 10.30 till 17.00 daily. Brass rubbing, plate rubbing.

Combe Martin Motor Cycle Collection. Near sea front. End May to end September daily 10.00 till 18.00. Early and late motor cycles and memorabilia.

Combe Martin Wildlife and Leisure Park. Alongside the A399. Manor house set in 15 acres of woodland with ornamental plants, birds, animals, play area.

Combe Sydenham Country Park, Monksilver. Off the B3168 between Watchet and Monksilver. April to end October Mon. to Fri. 10.00 till 17.00. House built 1585 (only court room open to view). 500 acre country park.

Combat Collection. Umberleigh, Barnstaple. April to October every day 10.00 till 18.00. Collection of 50 military vehicles.

Dartington Crystal, Torrington. Open most of the year. Manufacturers of lead crystal glass. Factory tours, shop.

Exmoor Bird Gardens, Bratton Fleming, near Barnstaple. Open all year except Christmas Day. April to October 10.00 till 18.00. November to March 10.00 till 16.00. Tropical birds, Tarzan Land.

Exmoor Natural History Centre, Malmsmead, off the A39 near County Gate. May to September, Wed. and Thur. (also Tue. in summer holidays). Displays, maps, geology, picnic area, guided walks.

Elliot Gallery, Braunton. Open Tue., Thu., Fri., Sat. Summer daily 10.00 till 18.00 and Winter 10.30 till 17.00.

Farm World, Bodstone Barton, off the B3343 near Berrydown Cross, Combe Martin. Easter to end October every day 10.30 till 18.00. Farm, collection of machines, implements. Walks and demonstrations.

Great Western Horseboat Company, Tiverton. Short distance from the town centre. Canal boat trips.

Glen Lynn Gorge, Lynmouth. Walk along a lovely tree lined gorge where there is also a small hydro electric power station.

Hinkley Point Nuclear Power Station. 8 miles North West of Bridgwater. All year Information Centre 10.00 till 16.00 (Sat. 10.00 till 14.00). 75 acre site on coast. Guided tours of reactor. Advance booking.

Hancock's Cider, South Moulton. Mon. to Sat. 9.00 till 13.00 and 14.00 till 17.30. Tours Easter to October. Five generations of cider making. Picnic area, craft shop, off-licence, film.

John Wood Sheepskin Tannery, Minehead. Craft centre and cafe all year 9.00 till 17.00 (Sat. 9.00 till 16.00). Factory tours Easter to October, Monday to Friday. Sheepskin made into rugs, toys, slippers.

Lynton and Barnstaple Garden Railway, Parracombe. Just off the A39 between Lynton and Blackmoor Gate. Easter to October 10.00 till 18.00 (closed Fri.). ¼ mile of railway track on bed of former Lynton and Barnstaple Railway. Adjoins ancient Saint Petrock's Church. Refreshments.

Minehead Shoe Factory, North Road, Minehead. Shop open Mon., to Fri. 9.00 till 17.00. (Sat. 9.00 till 12.00). Cooperative formed after Clarks closed. Watch production.

North Devon Leisure Centre, Barnstaple. Open every day. Sports hall, swimming pool, skittle alley, snooker, cafeteria, bar.

Quantock Sheep Milking Centre, New Stowey Farm, Nether Stowey. Just off the A39 between Bridgwater and Watchet. Milk a sheep, farm walks, walks.

Quince Honey Farm, South Moulton. Every day. Indoor apiary, cafe, picnic area, shop, honey and beeswax.

Rosemoor Garden, Great Torrington. 1 mile South East of Great Torrington on the B3220. Easter to October daily 10.00 till 18.00 (17.00 October). Royal Horticultural Society's internationally renowned garden. See a new garden in the making. Shop, restaurant.

Sheppey's Cider, Bradford-on-Tone, Taunton. On A38. May to September 8.30 till 19.00. October to April 8.30 till 18.00 Mon. to Sat. Also Sun. Easter to Xmas 12 till 14.00.

Somerwest World, Minehead. On the sea front. Mid April to mid October daily 10.00 till 19.00. Day visits to Butlin's leisure complex, funfair, swimming pool, cable car, lake.

Tarka Trail Cycle Hire, British Rail Station, Barnstaple. May to October 9.00 till 17.00. Also weekends March, April, November, December. Choice of routes along an old railway line beside the Taw and Torridge estuary.

Tropiquaria, Washford Cross, Watchet. On the A39 next to the radio masts. Where the tropics come to life. Indoor jungle, submarine crypt.

Watermouth Castle, Ilfracombe. On the B3343 near Woolacombe. Opens at various times April to October daily. Billed as one of the U.K.'s most exciting and unique all weather attractions.

NOTE

As well as attractions within Exmoor and the Quantocks, a number of others which are outside have been included if they are nearby and could be of interest when holidaying in the area. Ilfracombe, Taunton and Bridgwater are the three largest towns which lie just outside the area and have a range of attractions but no attempt has been made to list all of the attractions in these towns.

FAMILY WALKS SERIES

Family Walks in the Lake District. Barry McKay. ISBN 0 907758 40 1.

Family Walks in West Yorkshire. Howard Beck. ISBN 0 907758 43 6.

Family Walks in Three Peaks and Malham. Howard Beck. ISBN 0 907758 42 8.

Family Walks in South Yorkshire. Norman Taylor. ISBN 0 907758 25 8.

Family Walks in Cheshire. Chris Buckland. ISBN 0 907758 29 0.

Family Walks in the Staffordshire Peak and Potters. Les Lumsdon. ISBN 0 907758 34 7.

Family Walks in the White Peak. Norman Taylor. ISBN 0 907758 09 6.

Family Walks in the Dark Peak. Norman Taylor. ISBN 0 907758 16 9.

Family Walks in Snowdonia. Laurence Main. ISBN 0 907758 32 0.

Family Walks in Mid Wales. Laurence Main. ISBN 0 907758 27 4.

Family Walks in South Shropshire. Marian Newton. ISBN 0 907758 30 4.

Family Walks in the Teme Valley. Camilla Harrison. ISBN 0 907758 45 2.

Family Walks in Hereford and Worcester. Gordon Ottewell. ISBN 0 907758 20 7.

Family Walks in the Wye Valley. Heather and Jon Hurley. ISBN 0 907758 26 6.

Family Walks in the Cotswolds. Gordon Ottewell. ISBN 0 907758 15 0.

Family Walks in South Gloucestershire. Gordon Ottewell. ISBN 0 907758 33 9.

Family Walks in Oxfordshire. Laurence Main. ISBN 0 907758 38 X.

Family Walks around Bristol, Bath and the Mendips. Nigel Vile. ISBN 0 907758 19 3.

Family Walks in Wiltshire. Nigel Vile. ISBN 0 907758 21 5.

Family Walks in Berkshire and North Hampshire. Kathy Sharp. ISBN 0 907758 37 1.

Family Walks on Exmoor and the Quantocks John Caswell. ISBN 0 907758 46 0.

Family Walks in Mendip, Avalon and Sedgemoor. Nigel Vile. ISBN 0 907758 41 X.

Family Walks in North West Kent. Clive Cutter. ISBN 0 907758 36 3.

Ready Spring 1992

Family Walks in the Weald of Kent and Sussex
Family Walks in North Yorkshire
Family Walks around Luton and Dunstable
Family Walks in Northumbria
Family Walks in Nottinghamshire
Family Walks on the Isle of Wight
Family Walks in Clwyd
Family Walks in Dorset
Family Walks in Rossendale, Pendle and Bowland

Other titles under consideration

The Publishers, D. J. Mitchell and E. G. Power welcome suggestions for further titles in this Series; and will be pleased to consider other manuscripts of Derbyshire and regional interest from new or established authors.
